New Island, Falkland Islands
A South Atlantic Wildlife Sanctuary
for conservation management

New Island Conservation Trust

An independent conservation organisation

www.newislandtrust.com

ISBN 978-0-9550708-1-3

"A unique reserve for the protection of wildlife and environment, but where man can also find refuge to enjoy and study nature in a beautiful landscape.
A rare privilege that should continue by remaining free of board walks, notices, fences and following only common sense rules".

An observation by a much travelled German High Court Judge and guest,
New Island, 1977

Credits

Published by Design In Nature, Falkland Islands
2007
Designed by Georgina Strange
www.designinnature.com

Authors
Ian J. Strange MBE, with contributions by Dr Paulo Catry, Georgina Strange and Dr Petra Quillfeldt
Edited by Georgina Strange and Maria Strange

Photographic Credits
All photographs, unless otherwise stated, © G. Strange & I. J. Strange of Design In Nature
Photograph page 24 (top) & page 112 © Dan Birch www.danbirchphoto.com
Photograph (Sea Lion with penguin), page 72 © Nigel Winn www.island-expeditions.co.uk

Text Copyright © Ian J. Strange, 2007
New Island Map © G. Strange
Distribution Maps courtesy of and © Dr Paulo Catry
Map of the Falkland Islands & Fur seal line drawing © Ian J. Strange
Log Book Extracts courtesy of and © Nantucket Historical Society with thanks to Betsy Tyler

Thanks to Butler & Tanner Ltd., England for their high quality work and generous donation towards the printing of this document

Front & Back cover photos: (Front) New Island's South End beach; Yellow Daisies; Black-browed albatross & chick; Rockhopper penguins at sunset. (Back) Black-browed albatross
Previous page: A view over New Island looking south from Bold Hill
Opposite page: The Striated caracara's natural curiosity
All images © G. Strange

None of the photographs, maps or illustrations in this document may be copied or reproduced in any way without prior permission from the photographers/authors.

Photo: Red-backed Buzzard silhouette

Contents

Preface	1
An Introduction to the Contents	3
Acknowledgements	5
An Introduction to New Island	7
Early History 1774-1854: American Whalers and Sealers	11
Early History 1851-1949: Crown Land Leases	15
The New Island Project	19
Historical Sites	29
Natural Environment	31
Marine & Terrestrial Vegetation	39
Birds	45
Mammals	71
Non-native Species	75
Research Strategy	85
Environmental Management Policies	89
Conservation Policies	93
The Island's Infrastructure	99
From the Founder of the New Island Trust	109
Annexes 1-10	110
Map of the Falkland Islands	150
Map of New Island	151
New Island Conservation Trust Charity & Contact details	152

List of Annexes:

1) Captain Charles Barnard's Building, New Island, 1813: A History

2) Conservation and Environmental Monitoring Projects: New Island, 2006-2011

3) National Government Policies and International Commitments: Relevance of the Current Environmental Management Plan

4) An assessment of the possible impact of disturbance caused by tourists at the New Island South seabird colonies

5) Black-browed Albatross Population Census at New Island South, 2004 & 2006. Population Trends from 1977-2007

6) Distribution Maps, New Island South: Relative Abundance of Rabbits, 2004; Magellanic Oystercatchers with nests/broods, 2004/05

7) Research carried out on New Island South, 1975-2007

8) Published science papers, reports and books based on research conducted on the New Island reserve

9) Additional Bibliography and References

10) New Island's Code of Practice for Visitors

Photos: (this page) Upland goose
(opposite) A view over the south end of New Island

Preface

This work is not a conventional management plan, but an account of what New Island has experienced and an explanation for what we see today. Its aim is to answer many questions about the island, and to be a baseline and a pointer for future management. It presents some plans for the years to come, but it is hoped it will encourage those who follow to reflect a little on the island's past, before making judgement for its future.

New Island is quite unique, but not in the sense that it is pristine, for that feature was to disappear two centuries ago when its spoliation by man began. Ironically, this very spoliation has demonstrated the power of nature and its resilience to man's activities, and today the island is a living example of how its wildlife has survived some of the most incredible ravages. A few of these are documented in this work, but the true level of spoliation will probably never be known.

Some 35 years ago, a simple initiative was developed on New Island to try and re-balance the damage that man had done to it. The removal of sheep and cattle, the closure of egg collecting, prohibiting the shooting of wildlife and improved general husbandry were relatively simple to achieve; the politics behind trying to justify such actions and holding on to this initiative were less so.

Today the island is again one property under the ownership and management of this Trust. Its past adds another level to its unique quality; those who now come to view or work on the reserve have not one, but two living examples of environmental management and how man can assist in a re-balance with nature.

A lot of ground work has been carried out on the island, but by far the greatest changes have come about from the work of nature itself. Under the protection of the New Island Conservation Trust, these changes can continue into the future for the improvement of the island's environment and its exceptional wildlife.

Ian J Strange MBE
Originator of the New Island Conservation Trust
New Island, 2006

These conservation ideals were continued by the author, but were confined to the southern half of the island between 1986 and 2006, during which time the island was divided into two separate properties: New Island North and New Island South. The northern half of the island was run under new ownership and small-scale sheep farming was continued until 2004. It is important to recognise that nature conservation and tourism were also developed on the northern property, and a nature reserve was established, albeit in a different manner from the southern property. New Island South was further developed into a sanctuary for wildlife and a base for environmental research. The South reserve was placed under a private Trust, thus ensuring its protection for the future, and guaranteeing the continuation of its conservation projects.

Photos: (this page) Striated Caracara
(opposite) Scurvy Grass in flower

An Introduction to the Contents

When efforts were first made to compile what had been termed a management plan for the island, it rapidly became clear that no meaningful plan could be based simply on present day studies, nor could it follow a management profile for another site, even if that site was within the Falklands. Similarly, the plan could not be based solely on scientific data, when so much of the island's baseline is composed from "ground level values", simply; observations and working experience.

There was a need to include the findings of certain pieces of research work, but placing these in the main work would not have produced a readable format, which is an important aim of the publication.

The recent acquisition of the New Island North nature reserve from Tony and Kim Chater in September 2006, will eventually lead to more baseline information being added to publications on this section of the island. Due to commitments already made on the timing of publication, this work had to rely heavily on data originating only from the New Island South project.

The work is divided into two parts: the main descriptive section, which covers the island's history, conservation and research commitments, environmental makeup, wildlife, management and infrastructure; and a number of Annexes which include:

- A History of Captain Charles Barnard's Building
- Future Conservation and Environmental Projects
- National Government Policies and International Commitments
- Tourism Impact Assessment Study
- Black-browed Albatross Census & Long term Population Trends for New Island South
- Wildlife Distribution Maps
- Research carried out on New Island South, 1975-2007
- Published Science Papers, Reports and Books based on research carried out on New Island South
- Additional Bibliography and References
- New Island's Code of Practice for Visitors

Every aspect of New Island that was considered relevant to this work has been included here in this Management Plan, but it was not possible to include, for example, many published research papers covering work carried out on the reserve.
Some of these works, plus further information, photographs and links may be found on the New Island Conservation Trust website:

www.newislandtrust.com

New Island Conservation Trust
Memorandum and Legal Responsibilities

From The Chairman, Air Vice-Marshal David Crwys-Williams CB RAF (Ret'd)

The New Island Conservation Trust is a UK- registered charity that is governed by both the Charities Act 2006 and by Company law. As such it has a Board of Trustees who also act as Directors of the Limited Company.

Since its inception, the Trust has been blessed with a team of knowledgeable and industrious Trustees who give much time to the affairs of the charity.

Four of the Trustees are based in the United Kingdom and three in the Falkland Islands. They have diverse professional backgrounds, and have been appointed so that the Board has access to a wide range of expertise, experience and skills directly relevant to the charity, much of it at the highest international level.

The Trust's objects, as set out on the Memorandum and Articles of Association, are:
- To maintain and preserve for the benefit of the public the natural habitat and natural resources of New Island;
- The preservation and protection for the benefit of the public of buildings, monuments and structures forming part of the history of the island; and
- To advance the education of the public in the ecology, conservation, history, and other matters relating to New Island in particular by the provision of educational and study facilities.
- To secure the protection or preservation of the natural habitat, flora and fauna and environment for the protection of the wildlife and landscape and the conservation, refurbishment and preservation of buildings, monuments and structures which have featured in the history of the island, or which have been used or have played a part in the development of its industries including, but not limited to, the whaling industry;
- To provide educational and study facilities for visitors and more generally to promote the study and appreciation of ecology and conservation and any matters of historic, artistic, architectural or scientific interest.

The Trustees meet formally at least four times a year to discharge their duties of controlling the management and administration of the charity.
They recognise that they are legally responsible for the overall management and decision making in the charity. They are also responsible for the direction and performance of the charity. As a result the Trustees diligently monitor the Trust's income, expenditure, investments, property and other assets, and ensure that all required administration and formal reports are accurately collated and filed on time.
All trustees are involved in the taking of decisions and are aware of the importance of only acting in the best interests of the charity. The guiding principles are to act reasonably and prudently, ensuring that decisions are made within the provisions of the Memorandum and Articles of Association, and that professional advice is always sought when needed or required by law.

Acknowledgements

A number of individuals have been involved in putting material together for this document. In particular, the mapping and bird data of the present time, incorporated in the main work, is largely the work of Dr Paulo Catry, who also contributed to the fund-raising and planning aspects of the plan. Dr Catry also researched regulatory material of national and international importance for inclusion in the main text. Maria and Georgina Strange had the not so enviable nor easy task of editing and marrying together the varying text profiles. The photographs in this document are mainly the works of Georgina Strange and Ian Strange, with contributions from Dan Birch and Nigel Winn. Design and publishing was carried out in-house by Georgina Strange of Design In Nature.

Volunteers

The continuing success of the project and our ability to carry on with its operation has been made possible largely through the efforts of a large number of volunteers. Through the years they have come not just as field assistants or to study wildlife, but to help with the more mundane tasks such as fence clearance, rodent trapping, land management, building and general maintenance. The building of the reserve's infrastructure would not have been possible without the hard work of Harald and Hedel Voss, who with their yacht *Moritz-D* made New Island a home base for many seasons. Special thanks is also due to Gillian Walker for her promotional and volunteer work, and to the late Ingrid Schenk, who was inspired by the reserve to become a biologist and gave so much of her time working on the island. To all we extend our thanks.

Donations and Support

We are particularly indebted to the Geoffrey C Hughes Trust and John Young for their generous support, which resulted in the building of the reserve's Field Station, and the acquisition of New Island North in 2006.

It is with the support of a grant from the Overseas Territories Environmental Programme (OTEP), Foreign & Commonwealth Office, London, that we have been able to write up and publish this document.

Funding for long term scientific research, including full time personnel and equipment was granted to Dr Petra Quillfeldt and is thanks to the Deutsche Forschungsgemeinschaft, Germany. Thanks also to the NERC Stable Isotope Facility and the Falkland Islands Government (FIG). The FIG have also supported Dr Paulo Catry's research, and additional support is thanks to the Portuguese Science Foundation.

To all who have contributed to the New Island Conservation Trust, in any way, we are eternally grateful - with your help, New Island can continue as one of the South Atlantic's most valuable wildlife sanctuaries.

New Island Conservation Trust Board of Trustees

The New Island Conservation Trust as a Registered Public Charity has a board of trustees under the Chairmanship of Air Vice-Marshal David Crwys-Williams CB RAF (Ret'd). Trustees: Professor Sir Ghillean Prance MA Dphil Fil Dr FLS FiBiol FRGS, Margaret Butler, Phyllis M. Rendell, Captain Peter Erskine CBE RN (Ret'd), Jeffrey Mills TD FRGS, Darwin Lewis Clifton OBE, and secretary: Sarah Jones-Parry.
Dr Sheila Pankhurst, a founder trustee and secretary, but presently retired from the board, did much for the Trust's original founding.
Through the Trust and the dedication and voluntary work of the trustees, New Island will remain a reserve in perpetuity.

6

An Introduction to New Island

Since 1973, New Island has operated as a wildlife reserve and base for carrying out research on the natural environment. It is the only purpose designed site with such a long standing history of nature conservation in the Falkland Islands.

New Island is one of some fourteen islands in the Falkland archipelago which are settled - i.e. they have infrastructure supporting semi- or permanent populations. Originally a base for whalers and sealers in the late 1700s through to the mid 1800s, it was then run as a sheep farm for approximately 120 years.

When the project began in 1973, it was designed to operate at one of three positions depending on its development and financial viability. The first level involved the year-round occupation of the reserve, the second was its operation for six to eight months, and the final level was to leave the island as a closed reserve with only occasional visits to check progress. Presently the New Island (South) reserve and its facilities is operated at the central position.

During the period September through to April the reserve is fully occupied with its summer work. During the austral winter months of May, June, July and August when field work would be limited but costs of running the facility high, the infrastructure is closed down.

Geographical Position and General Description

New Island lies in the SW corner of the Falkland Islands and is one of a group of some thirty islands, which effectively create a small archipelago of their own.

Its position is 61°18' W and 51°43' S at the settlement, which lies at the approximate centre of the island.

The most westerly inhabited place of the Island group, it is located 147 miles (237 km) from Stanley, the capital, and approximately 220 miles (354 km) from the nearest point on the South American continent.

The island has roughly 52 miles (84 km) of coastline, is approximately 8 miles (12.8 km) in length and covers an area of approximately 2011 ha (5000 acres), (FIG Dept. of Agriculture, 2003).

The terrain is rugged and the highest peak (South Hill) reaches 743 feet (244m). Sheer cliffs dominate the western side of the island, while low ground predominates on the eastern shores, where several deep bays shelter a number of sandy beaches.

A Valuable Wildlife Sanctuary

New Island is home to more than forty different species of bird, including significant numbers of breeding Black-browed Albatross, Rockhopper penguins, Gentoo penguins and Striated Caracara, all of which are globally important in conservation terms, classing the island as an Important Bird Area.

The island holds the largest known breeding colony in the World of a small burrowing petrel, the Thin-billed Prion, with an estimated two million breeding pairs.

New Island also holds one of the Falklands' ten breeding colonies of Fur Seal, and the surrounding marine environment provides a rich feeding habitat for cetaceans such as Peale's Porpoise and the Killer Whale.

Photo opposite: Part of New Island's stunning coastline - the South End Beach

Photo above: Nesting Black-browed Albatross on New Island. Long-term aerial surveys of Black-browed albatross populations on New Island South have shown a steady increase over the 29 years that surveys have been made, and New Island continues to be an important breeding ground for these birds (see Birds section, Pg. 45, and Annex 5, for more details on census work and research).

The importance of New Island as a breeding site along with a number of other islands on this western side of the Falkland archipelago can be attributed to the Falkland Current. One of the main streams of this current flows up the west side of the island, creating some of the richest marine feeding grounds around the Falklands.

Photo above: New Island, and its surrounding islands of Coffin, Beef, Ship, Cliff Knob, Saddle and North, from the air. The contrast between New Island's steep, rugged terrain on its west coast, and the sheltered bays and harbours of its eastern side are shown here.
For a detailed map of New Island, please see Pg. 152.

New Island and Fakland Islands Oil Exploration

The geographical position of New Island is also important in other ways. In September 1995 an agreement was made between the British and Argentine Governments whereby an area of the SW Atlantic was designated as the Special Co-Operation Area (SCA). This area is positioned where the two 200-mile offshore territorial limits claimed by both countries overlap. Earmarked as a potential oil exploration area it is possible that at some point in the future the SCA will be licensed for oil exploration. New Island is the closest landfall to this Area, lying less than 60 miles (96 km) from its NE boundary.

Coffin Island, and a view towards Weddell Island from the east coast of New Island

Early History 1774-1854
American Whalers & Sealers

During research of old records and log books of American whalers and sealers, it became apparent that New Island featured a great deal. As this research continues and more information comes to light, so our knowledge of the island increases. Not only are we finding out how important the island was as a base to early American whalers, we are learning more about its environment in former times. This knowledge helps present day studies, explaining why certain aspects of the environment are like they are today.

To understand why it was that these American whalers and sealers came to use this particular area of the Falkland Islands, one has to look at events in America in the 1770s. The search for whale oil was clearly a primary reason, but it was also influenced by the War of Independence. The history surrounding these events is complex and is beyond the scope of this work. However some events were to have a direct bearing on the use of places like New Island by the American whale men and an attempt is made to detail these.

The War of Independence and Nantucket Whalers in the Falklands

The discovery of a new whaling ground off the Falkland Islands occurred in the early 1770s. Freeman in his "History of Cape Cod" states that the Cape Cod ships, in the year 1774, were the first to these grounds and that their voyages were made at the suggestion of Admiral Montague of the British Navy ("The Sea Hunters", Stackpole, 1953). Montague reported that he had sighted considerable numbers of whales off the Falklands at that time. However, it was written of the Nantucketeers in 1772 that they had by this year, already gone to the Falkland Islands.

By 1773-74 the small island of Nantucket was a prosperous Quaker enclave with whaling being their main occupation. At this time the Nantucket fleet numbered 150 ships and of the 2800 seamen out of that port, 2200 were whalers.

The "Boston Tea Party" Episode

In June 1773 the ships *Dartmouth* of New Bedford, owned by Francis Rotch, and the *Beaver* of Nantucket, owner William Rotch, captained by Hezekiah Coffin, took a cargo of sperm whale oil to London. Nantucket at this time traded closely with London. It was these ships that then returned with a cargo of 298 chests of tea for America, leading to Nantucket playing an unwilling part in what was to be a historical event referred to as the "Boston Tea Party". The new Colony rebels, angry at having taxes imposed on them by Britain for items such as tea, boarded the whale ships and threw the cargo overboard.

Following the news of The Boston Tea Party episode, the British Parliament brought out the coercive acts. The first one in March 1774 was the Boston Port Bill aimed at bottling up the "hot bed of New England rebels". The passage of the Restraining Act early in 1775, not only restricted the trade and commerce of Massachusetts, New Hampshire, Rhode Island and Connecticut to Britain, Ireland and the West Indies, but prohibited the colonial fishing on the Banks of Newfoundland, including whaling.

On 2 March 1775 the House of Commons was holding a hearing on the proposed "Fishery Bill", a law designed to cut Massachusetts off from its traditional use of the Grand Banks, as well as restraining its trade.

Captain Seth Jenkins of Nantucket appeared before the House to tell Parliament that Nantucket had 132 ships in the whale fishery alone and that 128 belonged to members of the Society of Friends called Quakers. At this hearing he stated they fished in all seasons and had recently extended whaling to the Falkland Islands. Many London merchants, together with David Barclay and several other prominent English Quakers, actually supported the Colonial cause. But arguments, facts and figures were in vain and the Restraining Act was passed.

Nantucket people, largely Quakers who did not believe in acts of war, were caught up in the revolution with severe results. Nantucket became designated as a loyalist stronghold and in September 1775, the General Court of Massachusetts, in issuing permits for vessels to go whaling, stipulated they must give a bond of £2,000 per vessel. Their cargoes were to be returned to some port in the Colony, Boston and Nantucket excepted.

There was no middle course for Nantucket's Quaker whale men. In order to sail they must accept the bond to obtain permits, or be judged Tories. If they were intercepted at sea by the British blockading fleet they would be seized as rebels. As their entire economy depended on whaling, the Quaker ship owners had no alternative but to continue and fit out their vessels to follow their trade.

A Secret Rendezvous - In the Falkland Islands

It was at this point that four prominent whale oil merchants conceived an idea which, they hoped, would salvage their industry until the troubles were resolved. These men were Francis Rotch of New Bedford and Nantucket, Richard Smith of Boston, Aaron Lopez of Newport and Leonard Jarvis of Dartmouth. Their plan was both bold and daring, the idea being to establish a secret rendezvous for their fleet far from the scene of impending war, at the Falkland Islands.

From a letter from Jarvis to Lopez dated 5 April 1775, it is clear that whaling around the Falklands had already been established by ships from Nantucket. That same month the whale ship *Amazon* captained by Uriah Bunker returned to Nantucket with the news of the discovery of the Brazil Banks and that the River Plate and the Falkland Islands were excellent migratory routes for whales.

Unfortunately there is little written evidence of exactly when the first whale ships visited the Falklands, but it is reasonable to assume this could have been some time between 1772 and 1774. Rotch, Smith, Jarvis and Lopez, by specifically naming the Falkland Islands as a place to establish a base, must have already been in possession of information as to the suitability of the Islands.

Sixteen whaling vessels are recorded as being sent to the Islands. The Falklands have many harbours, but the requirement to establish a secret rendezvous for this number of ships left few suitable sites.

New Island's Quaker Connection

That these whalers decided on New Island is evident by the large number of harbours, passages and islands in the vicinity which bear names closely associated with the Nantucket whale men.

Situated in the south west corner of the Falklands and forming a small archipelago, there are islands with names such as Pitt, Barclay, Quaker, Fox, Penn, Coffin, Beaver, Tea, Green, and Governor. New Island has a Coffin's Harbour and a Ship Harbour. There are other harbours and passages bearing names such as Friend Passage, Quaker Harbour, Chatham Harbour, States Harbour and Beaver Harbour.

"New Isle", as it was called in one of the oldest log books cited, a reference used by these early whalers when they made a discovery, became an important base and self-styled home for these early exploiters; a base hidden from the eye of authority for at least forty years.

British Authority

Britain first took possession of the Falkland Islands in 1765 when it established a settlement at Port Egmont on Saunders Island, West Falkland. In 1774 Britain took formal leave of the Islands with Spain maintaining a settlement at Port Soledad on East Falkland until 1806. Between 1806 and 1820 the Islands were abandoned by authority and left to whalers and sealers. After a brief re-settlement by the newly formed United Provinces of the Rio de la Plata, Britain again took possession of the Islands in January 1833.

Soon after, authority started its intervention on the whalers and sealers. The Falklands' first Governor, Moody, wrote of New Island being a rendezvous for American whalers and noted that "the fishery is carried out in great secrecy".

Captain Grey, of HMS Cleopatra, visited New Island in 1837 and recorded that an American whaler, the Hesper, no longer fit for sea was anchored as a storage depot for eggs (penguin and albatross) which were sold to other whalers.

In 1853, the depredations by whalers were again brought to the attention of the British Government. Governor Rennie reported that whalers lying at New Island caught not only whales, but also seals. However, it appears that whales were becoming scarce and in 1854 a whaler reported that in the eight months they had been at New Island, only one whale had been caught.

Although the Falklands was well established under British sovereignty by 1850, its status was either unknown or casually ignored by foreign whaling and sealing crews. This led to an incident having far-reaching effects between the United States and Great Britain.

In early January 1854 six deserters from the American whaler Hudson and her tender Washington, appeared in Stanley, having come from New Island in a boat stolen from one of these vessels.

In a statement given to the magistrate they described how the Hudson, based at New Island, served as a depot for the Washington, which was employed to capture whales within the headlands of the Islands. Part of their statement read:
"That while so employed, Captain Clift (Hudson) and Eldridge (Washington) had killed a large number of hogs belonging to the Falkland Islands Company on Saunders Island and likewise destroyed a large number of seals on the Government rookeries."
They also stated that for about eight months the crew amounting to thirty six men, had

lived entirely on pork and geese killed on the Islands.

As a result, the Colonial Manager of the Falkland Islands Company took out a warrant for the arrest of Captains Clift and Eldridge on a charge of pig killing. The HMS Express with the Chief Constable aboard was despatched to New Island to arrest the two vessels and bring them to Stanley.
However, the news of the arrests had reached the American Consul in Montevideo who immediately despatched the corvette *Germantown* to Stanley to defend his countrymen.
The *Germantown*, a vessel of 1000 tons, with an impressive armament of cannons, far outmatched the 360 ton *HMS Express* and her six 32 pound cannons. The *Germantown's* arrival in Stanley was, according to Governor Rennie, met with some alarm. Seeing that the *Washington* and *Hudson* were under arrest, Captain Lynch of the American corvette "beat to quarters and shotted his guns". Rennie wrote that "this in sight and hearing of a small settlement totally defenceless naturally created alarm to the inhabitants" (Letter Books, FIG Archives, research I. J. Strange).

Captain Clift was brought to Court and fined, but the incident was to continue with letters passing from the United States Secretary of State to the British Minister at Washington. Some doubt as to the British Sovereignty over the Falklands was expressed and Britain's regulations of fishing about the Islands were questioned.

This event probably led to the eventual closure of New Island as a base for American whalers. Entries in the log books of American whaling vessels show that the island remained an important anchorage for some years to come. However, no doubt encouraged by the new British administration, the island was to become the scene of new ventures.

Below: A section from the Log books of the brig 'Aurora', with reference to collecting eggs from "the great Penguin rookery" on New Island, 3 November 1820

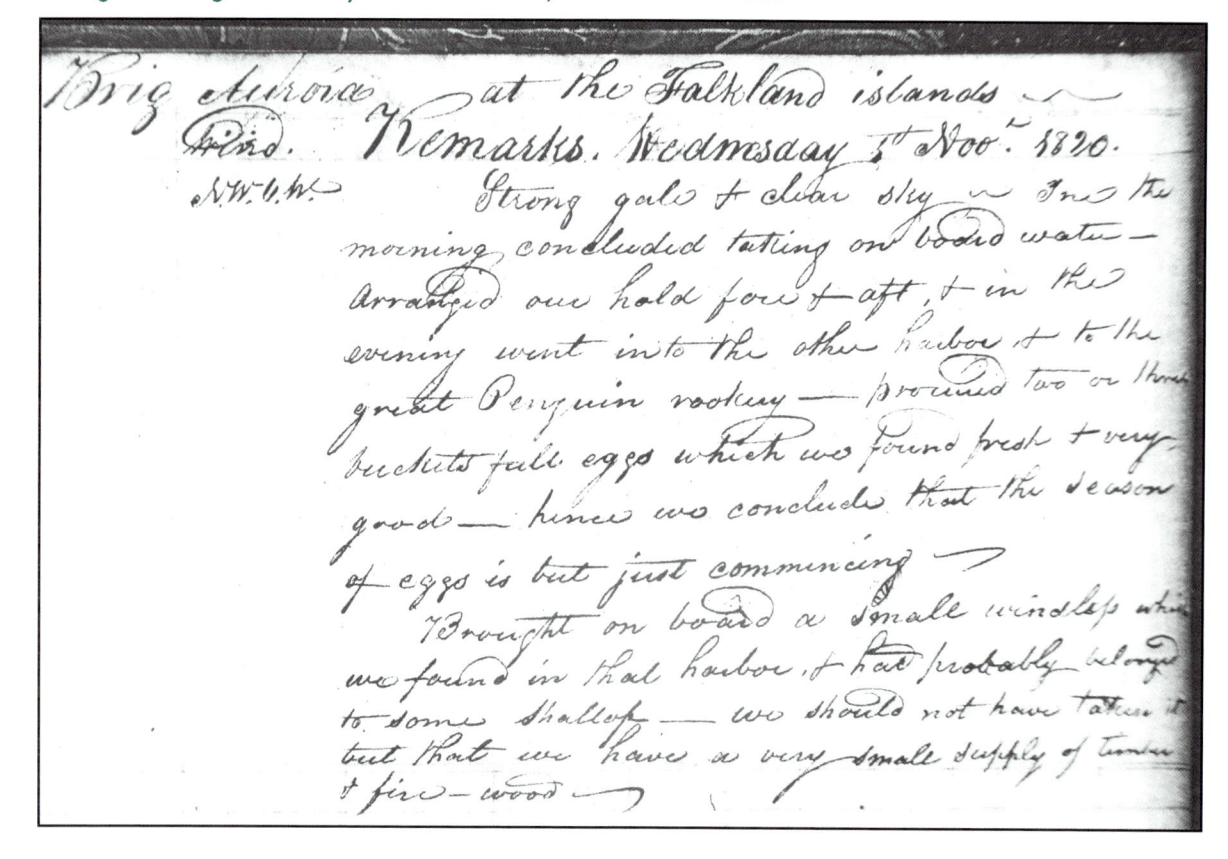

Early History 1851-1949
Crown Land Leases

New Island was the first area of land to be officially settled and stocked on West Falkland. It was also the only site in the archipelago of a Guano industry and land-based whaling factory.

Originally, after the settlement of the Falkland Islands by Great Britain in 1833, all the land on New Island was vested in the Crown. There is no direct evidence in the form of official documents that the Crown parted with any of New Island on agricultural lease before 1860. However, it appears highly likely that a lease for the entire island was granted before that year to Smith Brothers & Company, a River Plate Trading firm of Montevideo. Their official Crown Grant No 140, dated 3 May 1860 was for 160 acres (Attorney General, FIG, letter dated 4 January 1988).

It is apparent from the Grant's plan and map, that the area leased was the land occupied by the present settlement. The Smith Brothers Grant was the only grant of freehold made on New Island before 1895 which appears in the Register Book.

The Guano Industry, Sealing, Penguin Oiling and Sheep Farming on New Island

In 1851 Captain Campbell of the vessel *Levenside* obtained a licence from the Falkland Islands Government to investigate the deposits of guano on New Island, which was then owned by the Crown.

Guano was collected from the large penguin and albatross colony that is now known as the Settlement rookery, and was taken by pack horses to Levenside Cove, where a jetty and settlement had been established. Although Levenside Cove is not marked on any published maps, a copy of a painting made in the 1860s depicts the present Protector Beach with a rough stone jetty and what is today known as the Barnard Building.

The industry was very short lived, the guano found to be of very low quality and the *Levenside* sank afer striking a rock while entering Port William with her second cargo of guano.

At some point between 1851 and 1860, New Island was the site of another industry. A French brig, the *Victor* is recorded as having gone to New Island to collect "trypots etc". (Letter Books, FIG Archives, research I. J. Strange). Records are not specific about the type of oil taken or if indeed this venture was official and licensed.

The Smith Brothers lease gave rights to collect guano and oil, and to fish the coasts; an early reference to sealing. It is recorded that the firm sent their brig *Tigre* to "found a settlement at New Island", and that sheep, cattle and settlers were left on the island. Unfortunately the exact date is not recorded, but it would have been after 1851 and before 1860. What is evident, is that New Island was the first area of land to be settled and stocked on West Falkland.

Around late 1867/early 1868 Messrs. Bertrand and Switzer, who were interested in the prospects of acquiring land in the Falkland Islands, met an agent of the Smith Brothers in Montevideo. For the sum of £2,500 the Smith Brothers conceded their lease on New Island, including the 160 acres purchased from the Crown, to Bertrand and Switzer. Later a third partner, Mr Holmsted, joined in on the venture. The Smith Brothers lease still had 12 years to run and with this concession came about 4,000 sheep, some horses and two goats.

However the venture on New Island, for these partners, was already being replaced by their plans to take over a much larger holding on the mainland of West Falkland and in late 1869, most of the sheep were taken from New Island.

Holmested re-visited New Island in May 1872. He found the property had been occupied by visiting sealers and was in a bad state generally. This visit lasted three weeks when the remaining sheep were rounded up and shorn (M. Trehearne, 1978).

The land included in the Smith Brothers Grant changed hands several times, until on 13 July 1883 it was conveyed by J. M. Dean to E. Nilsson.

The island saw a succession of owners engaged mainly in sheep farming, although for a brief period in 1893 and 1894, Edward Nilssen was granted a "Sealing Licence" for the taking of 10,000 penguins. The remains of penguin corrals, circular walls of stone into which penguins were herded, on the Settlement rookery indicate that it was Rockhopper penguins which were taken for their oil. This was the last record of penguin oiling in the Falkland Islands.
The Scott Grant was made on 29 October 1919 when Fanny Maria Scott either bought out E. Nilssen or acquired possessory title to his land.

The next entry is a sale by the Trustees of Fanny Maria Scott on 16 September 1949 when New Island was passed to John J. Davis.

A New Whaling Venture

On 24 December 1905 two whale catchers and a floating factory ship, the *Admiralen,* anchored at New Island. These ships were owned by Norwegian Christen Christensen. A few days previously, the expedition manager, Alex Lange, had obtained permission from the Governor of the Falkland Islands to whale in the waters around the Falklands and to use New Island as a base.
"The arrival of the whalers on New Island on Christmas Eve 1905 was little short of a sensation for the only two isolated families living there, two widows with small children who ran a sheep farm" (the two widows were Mrs Larsen and Mrs Cull). There is mention of sheep numbering 2,100. The *Admiralen* remained at anchor for a month, during which time 40 whales were caught. The whalers then moved to South Georgia.

On 27 February Lange was once again back at New Island, where whaling brought in Sei whales only. Early in April 1906 the *Admiralen* left New Island bound for Sandefjord, Norway. Although a new licence was negotiated for the following season, the expedition did not return to New Island but directed their operations around South Georgia.

New Island's Whaling Station

In 1908 New Island became the site of a further attempt at whaling in the Falklands, when a lease was obtained by Messrs. Salvesen & Co of Leith, Scotland, for the operation of the first and last land-based whaling station in the Islands. Erected in South Harbour, the New Island whaling station was a fairly large operation, with a factory employing some eighty men. The facilities included Government buildings for a resident customs officer and a post office. In 1916 the station was closed and moved to South Georgia.

Photo above: Men flensing a whale at New Island's whaling station during the time that it was operational between 1908 & 1916. Photo right: The site of the station as it is today - old pieces of machinery, such as this steam-driven boiler, still exist as a reminder of this exploitative industry

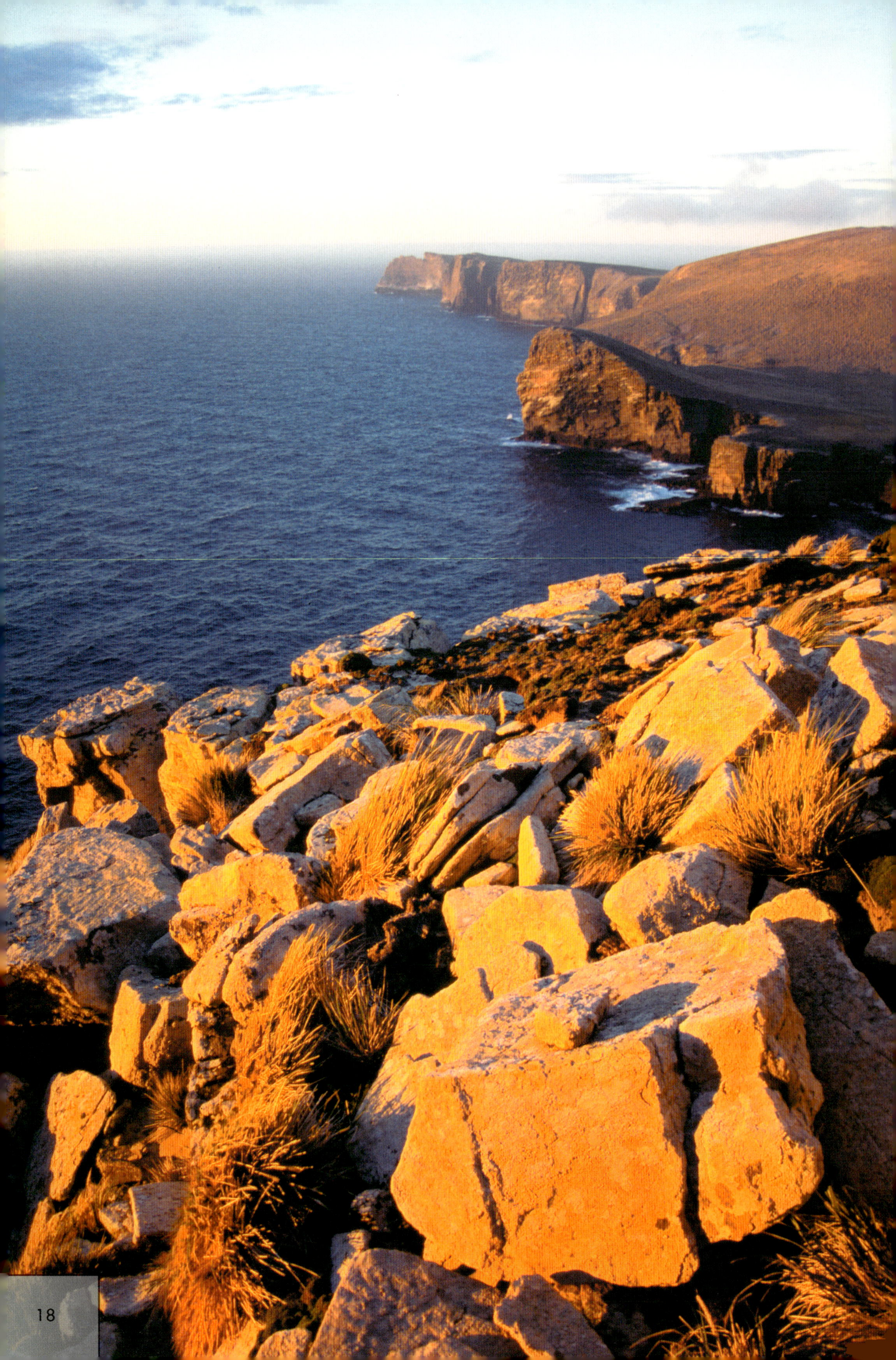

The New Island Project

The New Island Project was conceived in 1972 with the formation of the New Island Preservation Company by two conservationists, Roddy Napier and Ian Strange, with the help of Annie Gisby. In a predominantly staunch sheep farming community, the plan to turn New Island into a wildlife reserve, and to introduce wildlife research and eco-tourism to show their potential as forms of diversification for the Falklands, was a bold one. Its development was slow, marred by politics and costly legal proceedings to uphold its rights, but the objective has never changed. Today New Island, its original project and the research carried out on the reserve are recognised internationally, and under the New Island Trust, the island will be protected in perpetuity.

The Formation of the New Island Preservation Company - 1972

On 22 February 1972 the heir of John J. Davis, Raymond Davis, made a sale agreement with R. B. Napier for the purchase of New Island. On 19 May 1972 R. Davis conveyed New Island to the New Island Preservation Company Ltd (NIPCO) including the adjacent small islands of Coffin, Beef, Cliff Knob, Ship, Saddle, North Island and Landsend Bluff. The property was transferred to NIPCO on 30 January 1973.

There were two main shareholders of the New Island Preservation Company: R. B. Napier and I. J. Strange, each holding equal shares. The Company Memorandum was to establish the island as a wildlife reserve; to encourage conservation and research; and to develop specialised wildlife tourism. A small number of sheep were retained as part of the project to demonstrate the viability of the different schemes working together.

On 30 December 1973, as a gesture of its conservation intent and a precaution against the company going into liquidation with the potential loss of valuable conservation assets, its six offshore islands and the Landsend Bluff were transferred to the Society for the Protection of Nature Reserves (SPNR), (later to be called the Royal Society for Promotion of Nature Conservation). The agreement being with its founder, Christopher Cadbury, that when the New Island project was firmly established, these islands would be passed back. Negotiations for this were taking place when Mr Cadbury's untimely death resulted in the loss of the original understanding and the islands were transferred to Falklands Conservation.

The Beginning of Tourism and Wildlife Conservation

Specialised wildlife tourism started on New Island in 1973 and was the first such project in the Falkland Islands. In the same year limited conservation research started with two field researchers from Europe.

The New Island project worked well, but was marred by commercial tourism interests from outside.
In order to uphold the original project idea and the memorandum of the company, the

Photo above: A small group of tourists enjoying New Island in the 1970s
Opposite: New Island's spectacular west cliffs

originator, Ian Strange, applied to the Courts for NIPCO to be wound up; this took place in 1976. By agreement of the two shareholders the Court made the unusual ruling that the company assets be shared, rather than sold. This led to the land and its fixtures being divided rather than sold on the open market.

Photo above: Moving wool bales, 1973 - for a short time, sheep farming was continued by the NIPCO

The Property Division - 1978

From 1978 the island became two separate properties: New Island North and New Island South. New Island North was leased by its owner, Roddy Napier, and sheep farming continued on that property.

Under the ownership of Ian Strange, New Island South continued with the original project and the remaining sheep were removed completely from this part of the island. Management of the land continued as a key factor, with re-planting of native vegetation to further halt erosion, the control of introduced species and the removal of fencing. Environmental research continued to develop, and eco-tourism was advanced, with small groups of visitors from Europe and the USA.

The Founding of the Falkland Islands Foundation on New Island 1979

In the process of developing conservation ideals for New Island, some events and discussions on the island in 1979 led to a small group of people writing up and signing a memorandum for the creation of a conservation organisation.

This group of conservationists, namely Sir Peter Scott, Richard Fitter, Michael Wright, Marcus Stauffacher, Ian Strange and Maria Strange, had as the original purpose, the securing of funds for the New Island project. The Falkland Islands Foundation, later to become Falklands Conservation, was thus conceived on the island.

Photos below: Then and now - a comparison between the extreme erosion that existed on the island even twelve years after the removal of stock in this area (left), and the rich vegetation that can be seen in the same area today (right)

The Sale of New Island North - 1986

In 1986 New Island North, with stock, was sold by Roddy Napier to Tony Chater. Badly drafted documents following the winding up of the New Island Preservation Company resulted in a further Court hearing in December 1992 when the rights of both landowners were defined. Sheep farming, on a much reduced basis, continued on the New Island North property for some years. The property became a private nature reserve and sheep on this part of the island were finally removed in 2004.

The New Island South Conservation Foundation - 1986

In 1986, Ian Strange and family established a private trust, the New Island South Conservation Foundation, to ensure the continuation of the reserve's projects in perpetuity. In 1988, with the invaluable help of Dianne Prescott, the New Island Wildlife Conservation Foundation was established as a registered charity in the USA as a sister organisation.

Sanctuary Status for New Island South - 1993

In 1993 New Island South was given official Falkland Islands Government status as a Wildlife Sanctuary, later to be designated a National Nature Reserve in 1999.

The New Island South Conservation Trust - 1995

To strengthen further the continuation of the New Island South project, Ian Strange founded the New Island South Conservation Trust, a UK Registered Public Charity, on 18 May 1995. This Trust has a board of Trustees made up of members resident in the Falkland Islands and in the UK.

Photos above & left: Many species of bird such as Thin-billed prions (above) and Striated caracaras (left) were persecuted before the creation of the reserve on New Island. When the NIPCO took over management in 1973, the island saw its first step towards environmental protection. Now, 35 years later, New Island is home to more than 2 million pairs of prions - the largest breeding population in the world - and over 80 adult pairs of Striated caracaras.

Past Management

Prior to the New Island Preservation Company taking over the island in the summer of 1972/73, the property had been operated continually as a sheep farm for over 120 years.

Few records exist to show the levels of stocking when sheep farming first began on the island, but the earliest record is of approximately 4,000 sheep in 1868. There were 2,100 sheep in 1905. NIPCO took over 3,300 sheep, a number of cattle and horses. The island was heavily overgrazed at that stage, with very serious soil erosion in many areas. It had been practice to burn off native vegetation such as fern (*Blechnum magellanicum* and *Blechnum penna marina*) and Diddle-dee shrub (*Empetrum rubrum*) and to sow Yorkshire Fog (*Holcus lanatus*) as a replacement. In many areas, burning had led to further soil erosion through the loss of native plants.

Photo above: Sheep and cattle heavily overgrazed the island's vegetation pre-1973
Photo right: The same area today - dense vegetation now covers most of the valley, providing habitat for geese and small ground-nesting birds such as the Falkland Pipit

It was also common practice to gather penguin and albatross eggs, both as a form of subsistence and as a source of income. Many species of wildlife were viewed as being in direct conflict with sheep farming interests and were destroyed. Pigs had been brought in and allowed to run wild, in order to root out the burrows of ground nesting prions.

When new management was put in place by the New Island Preservation Company, an immediate priority was to arrest soil erosion caused by the overgrazing of sheep and the actions of pigs. All pigs were shot and the 3,300 sheep reduced immediately to about 1,500.

The shooting of wild birds and the collection of their eggs was banned, but local politics and the need to bring in some revenue saw the continuation of sheep farming for some four years. The plan to run New Island as a reserve, diversify into specialised wildlife tourism and conservation research was paramount. Efforts were therefore directed at removing all farming practices and to achieving these goals.

Below: Settlement Rookery - 1970s: Large areas of Tussac grass surrounding the main seabird colony on New Island south were grazed by cattle, causing widespread erosion

Below: Settlement Rookery - 2007: Tussac has now re-vegetated these areas, and many other species of plant, such as Wild Celery and Blue couch-grass, are now prolific

Current Ownership and Legal Status

On 26 August 1998, Ian Strange transferred the property known as New Island South to the New Island South Conservation Trust, retaining rights for himself and his family to live and work on the island.

The northern half of the island, which had been under separate ownership since 1986, was purchased by the Trust in May 2006. The whole island is now under NISCT ownership and is run as a reserve by Ian Strange under the original memorandum. In October 2006 the NISCT was renamed and is now the New Island Conservation Trust.

In 2007 the management of the island continues to follow the original "New Island Project" with the added advantage of a sound baseline developed from 35 years of practical experience, together with much improved infrastructure.

Photos: New Island's dramatic west cliffs with a view to Rookery Hill at dusk (above); and the view from Precipice cliffs, looking towards the North end of the island & Cathedral Cliffs (below)

The southern half of New Island remains a Falkland Islands Government (FIG) National Nature Reserve. However, the FIG does not play any role in the management of the reserve, although it has given some financial support, and still supports the Trust with small amounts to assist a number of management and research projects.

Photo above: Miguel Lecoq at the Settlement Rookery

Offshore Island Property

The original New Island Project has the distinction of having created six of its original island holdings as nature reserves, and although, due to unforeseen circumstances, these islands were lost as part of the property (see page 19), they continue to be protected areas. The NICT does however own three small islets known as Seal Rocks, which were passed to the Trust under a Crown Grant dated 21 September 2000.

Seal Rocks comprise three small islets located south of New Island, in Grey Channel. These rocky islets are partly covered with Tussac and aerial observations reveal that they are used as a haul-out site by Sea Lions, but we have little information on the fauna and flora of this site, as it is difficult to access.

Photo below: Yellow Daisy (Senecio littoralis)

Life and Work on the New Island Reserve

A Research Base

Commencing in late September and continuing until late March each year, New Island becomes an important base for the study of wildlife and the natural environment. On the reserve, all work is geared to this conservation and study of the environment, from our scientific projects through to controlled tourism and education.

Since the development of field studies on the South reserve, many studies have been carried out on the island's diverse fauna and flora, including native and introduced species.

The nature of our studies varies from the simplicity of counting numbers, to the most advanced technologies in scientific research, such as using satellite tracking devices on penguins.

The island's value as a natural outdoor laboratory for environmental sciences provides us with the perfect base to concentrate on a direct and more practical hands-on approach to nature conservation. As a permanent study site, a lot of our work concentrates on those species found in this particular island environment. This is also expanded to look closely at how geological makeup, vegetation, introduced species and changes in weather patterns may affect species ecology.

As an independent operation with a small administration, emphasis is placed on maintaining a high level of research using non-invasive, small-scale studies to minimize impact on both the site and species under survey.

Current Research Projects: 2006/07
During the 2006/07 field season, a variety of long-term conservation projects have been under way: Dr Petra Quillfeldt, currently in her third season of this project on New Island, is carrying out a seven-year, detailed behavioural and ecological study of Thin-billed prions on the reserve.

Working in Dr Quillfeldt's team are Dutch PhD student Riek van Noordwijk, who is studying various aspects of the ecology of King Cormorants; and Maud Poisbleau, carrying out a postdoctoral study on the behavioural ecology of Rockhopper Penguins. Research on these two species will continue until at least 2009.

Dr Paulo Catry, from Portugal, is in charge of an on-going project monitoring population dynamics, breeding and behavioural ecology of Black-browed Albatrosses on the reserve. Assisted by Rafael Matias, Miguel Lecoq, and PhD student Orea Anderson, this work will provide valuable data on this globally endangered species. The 2006 season was the fourth year of this project.
Additional research is being conducted by Dr Catry monitoring the breeding population of Striated caracaras on the island.

Many of the research and conservation projects carried out on New Island are important not just within the context of the Falkland Islands, but also within a global context. Data gathered from these studies, coupled with the habitat protection that the reserve provides, it is hoped that progress can be made towards a better understanding and further conservation of these species.

For more detailed information on New Island's conservation projects, please see the following sections: Birds (page 45), Non-native Species (page 75), Research Strategy (page 85) and Annex 2.

Tourism Today

Land-based tourism continued on New Island south until the Falklands War in 1982. After this, higher priority was given to research projects and conservation. Restrictions on air travel between New Island and Stanley presently also limit possibilities for visitors to the reserve.

However, New Island is currently one of the major destinations in the Falkland archipelago for visiting cruise ships. Ship-borne visitors to the reserve experience the bird life at the Settlement rookery, and also visit the newly completed Visitors Centre and Museum (for more detail on the Museum and its history, see Annex 1). Maintaining only small-scale eco-tourism remains paramount, and cruise vessels carrying more than approximately 160 passengers are not permitted to visit the island, in order to control the impact on the island's environment and its wildlife.

Photos: MS Hanseatic anchored in Settlement Harbour (above); Passengers come ashore on Protector Beach and visit the Captain Barnard Museum & Visitors Centre (below)

The remains of a steam-driven piece of machinery at New Island's old whaling station

Historical Sites

The preservation of historical buildings and sites on New Island is an important aspect of the Trust's work, and the island has a very rich and interesting past. It was the site of the first and only land-based whaling factory to be established in the Falkland Islands, and the recently restored Barnard Building stands as a monument to the trials of marooned whaling captain, Charles H. Barnard, in the early 1800s.

Evidence of New Island's rich history is clearly visible today in the buildings, sites and artefacts that remain. The two most prominent are The Barnard Building, now fully restored as a museum and visitors' centre, and the remains of a 1908 whaling station.
Dating from the 1880s is a building known as The Stone Cottage, which is of historical value and merits restoration. Of less value, but of interest is the Shearing Shed.

The Barnard Building

The Barnard Building, the origins of which go back to 1812 when Captain Charles Barnard was marooned on New Island with some of his crew, is without question one of the most important historical buildings on New Island, and in the Falkland Islands.

The story of Barnard's marooning is well documented in his book "Marooned - A Narrative of the Sufferings and Adventures of Capt. Charles H. Barnard, 1812-1816." (1829).
This historic building is now finally restored and has been named the Captain Barnard Museum and Visitors Centre. Now housing artefacts of the early American whaling period and other items of historical value, it also serves as a valuable interpretive centre, offering visitors to the island information about the reserve, its wildlife, and conservation work.

The building is a valuable asset to the Trust and offers an extra attraction to tourist vessels that call at New Island. Positioned at the head of a beach normally used for landing ship-bourne tourists, it is in an ideal location. The building will also include a small sales point offering tourists the opportunity to purchase and browse books, to view art prints and to obtain information about the Trust. For more information on the Barnard Building and its history, see Annex 1.

Whaling Station

The remains of the Salvesen & Co. Whaling Station of 1908-1916 are still visible in South Harbour. No buildings remain, but foundations and pieces of machinery exist to indicate the extent of the station, the only one to be built in the Falkland Islands.

Efforts have been made to better document what is present and to assess if there are specific needs for restoration. However, any form of restoration would be too costly and logistically difficult for the NICT alone.

Some smaller artefacts from the station, suitable for display in the Barnard Building Museum and Visitor Centre, have been moved from the site.

Whale bones are commonly found along the shores of New Island, a reminder of the whaling era. In general these are left in situ, in part for their aesthetic value and for visitors to view and photograph as part of the landscape, but they do present a dilemma in that, if left they will eventually break down and be lost. As a compromise, particularly attractive specimens have been collected for housing in the Barnard Building.

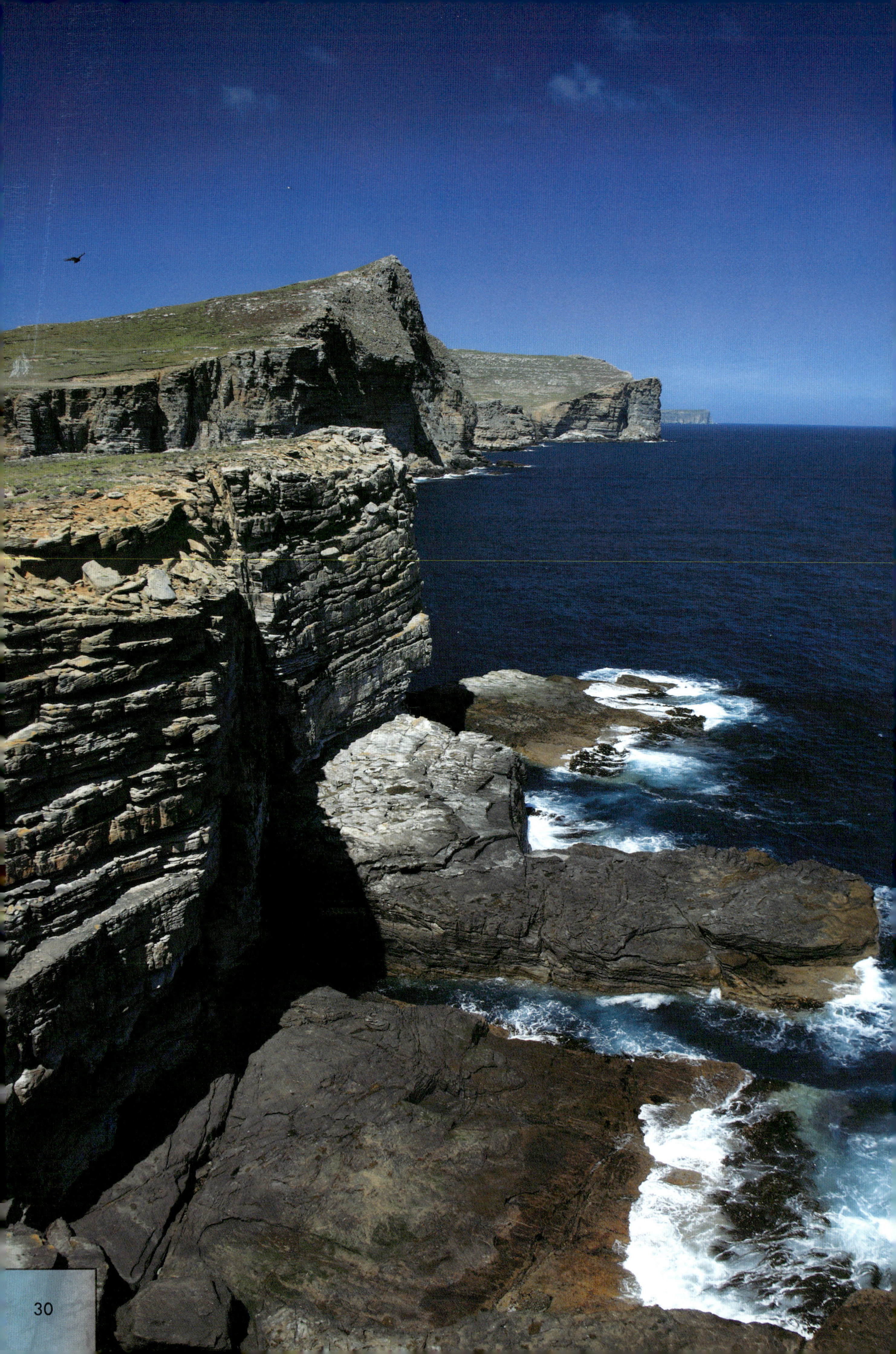

Natural Environment

New Island is possibly one of the most visually dramatic and picturesque islands in the Falkland archipelago in terms of its natural environment. Sheer sea cliffs rise to over 700 feet on its western face, and deep blue-green sheltered bays with wide sand beaches dominate its eastern shores.

Climate

The Falkland Islands have a cool, temperate oceanic climate featuring exceptionally changeable weather. There are important inter-island variations in climate parameters, particularly regarding cloud cover, solar radiation and precipitation. Winds are a common feature and frequent all the year round. Dominated by westerlies, there is often a noticeable difference between conditions on the west side of the archipelago and those on the east.

New Island, lying in the extreme west of the Falkland Islands, generally experiences more hours of sunshine and slightly higher temperatures than Mount Pleasant Airport on East Falkland. The mean average temperature for the summer months of December and Janurary 2006/07 on New Island was 10.6°C. In the winter months of June, July and August 2006 the mean was 4.7°C; slightly higher than that recorded at the Mount Pleasant Meteorological Office.

Rainfall
New Island has a very low annual rainfall; the average for the eight years between 1998 and 2006 being only 454mm. This is significantly less than recorded at Mount Pleasant.
Usually the main rainfall on New Island is during the winter months, however, in the period from March 2006 to March 2007, an exceptional rainfall of 518mm was recorded, with nearly half of this figure falling during the summer months of November to February.

Geology, Geomorphology, Soil and Water Resources

Geology
Relatively little work has been done on the geology of New Island. A number of geologists have at different times visited the island, but generally these have been by short term visitors and time has not allowed for in depth studies to be carried out. Dr Don Aldiss of the British Geological Survey made a visit of some four days in January 1997. It is from his investigations that most of the following is known.

In geological terms New Island belongs to the West Falkland Group which is dominated by sandstones, with some siltstones and mudstones. These sedimentary sequences are of the Silurian to Devonian ages, an average age being 400 million years. This West Falkland Group is made up of four formations, these formations are then divided into seven members representing both marine and fluvial environments.

Geology - Northern New Island
Two of these members, the Mount Alice Member and the South Harbour Member, which are both newly recognised subdivisions of the Port Stephens Formation are the main components of the New Island geology. The Mount Alice Member and the South Harbour Member represent contrasting facies. The latter was deposited in a fluvial environment, lacks trace fossils, is composed of coarse, more feldspathic deposits and is dominated by large scale trough cross bedding.

Photo opposite: Sea cliffs on New Island's western coastline

The South Harbour Member is mainly composed of medium and coarse grained subarkosic sandstones and forms the northern end of New Island.

West Cliff Formations

Folding and faulting strongly influenced landforms, and in the region of gently dipping resistant strata of the Port Stephens Formation, erosion on joints and dykes was to strongly influence the geology of the SW including New Island. Especially on coasts facing away from the direction of dips, the extensive subvertical cliffs, a feature of the island's west coast, are penetrated by steep-sided gullies. Intersecting joint sets give rise to such notable cliffs, especially such as those on the west facing slopes of North Bluff. Here, east-west striking joint sets dipping between 55 degrees to the north and 55 degrees to the south have intersected with each other and with north-north-westerly joints parallel to the coast, have formed a distinctive series of triangular-shaped ridges and gullies known as the Cathedral Cliffs.

Geology - Southern New Island

The Mount Alice Member is composed mainly of medium to coarse sandstones, some with trace fossils of a variety of types, and forms the southern part of New Island. In contrast to the northern section, the geology of the southern part of New Island was influenced by a marine environment and not a fluvial environment.

Fossils

Several types of trace fossils are found in the Mount Alice Member. The most common types are varieties of sub-horizontal vermiform burrows. On New Island there are at least two forms of these burrows. Examples of these can be seen as raised ridges which cross-cut in outcrops of very hard rock in the South End Tussac region.

On the south eastern facing beaches, pieces of petrified bone from unknown species of cetaceans have also been found. One of these remnants has the very characteristic shape and appearance of the upper section of a beaked whale skull. These bones vary in density, the heaviest pieces resembling polished marble. Others are lighter, retain the surface texture of bone and appear to be in a transition stage of fossilization.

Raised Beaches

Several remnants of raised beaches can be found on the island, one notable area is situated on the coast to the south east of New Island's airstrip, and another may be found on slopes of the west coast side of the South End Tussac area. A very large area also exists not far from the North End beach. These sites have yielded interesting collections of pebbles and small cobbles that are not related to the geology of the Islands.

For further information, see: "The Geology of the Falkland Islands", D. T. Aldiss & E. J. Edwards, British Geological Survey, 1999.

Photo above: An example of sub-horizontal vermiform burrows - a type of trace fossil quite commonly found on New Island south
Photo opposite: The spectacular formation of Precipice Cliffs which rise to over 700ft, on the west coast of the island

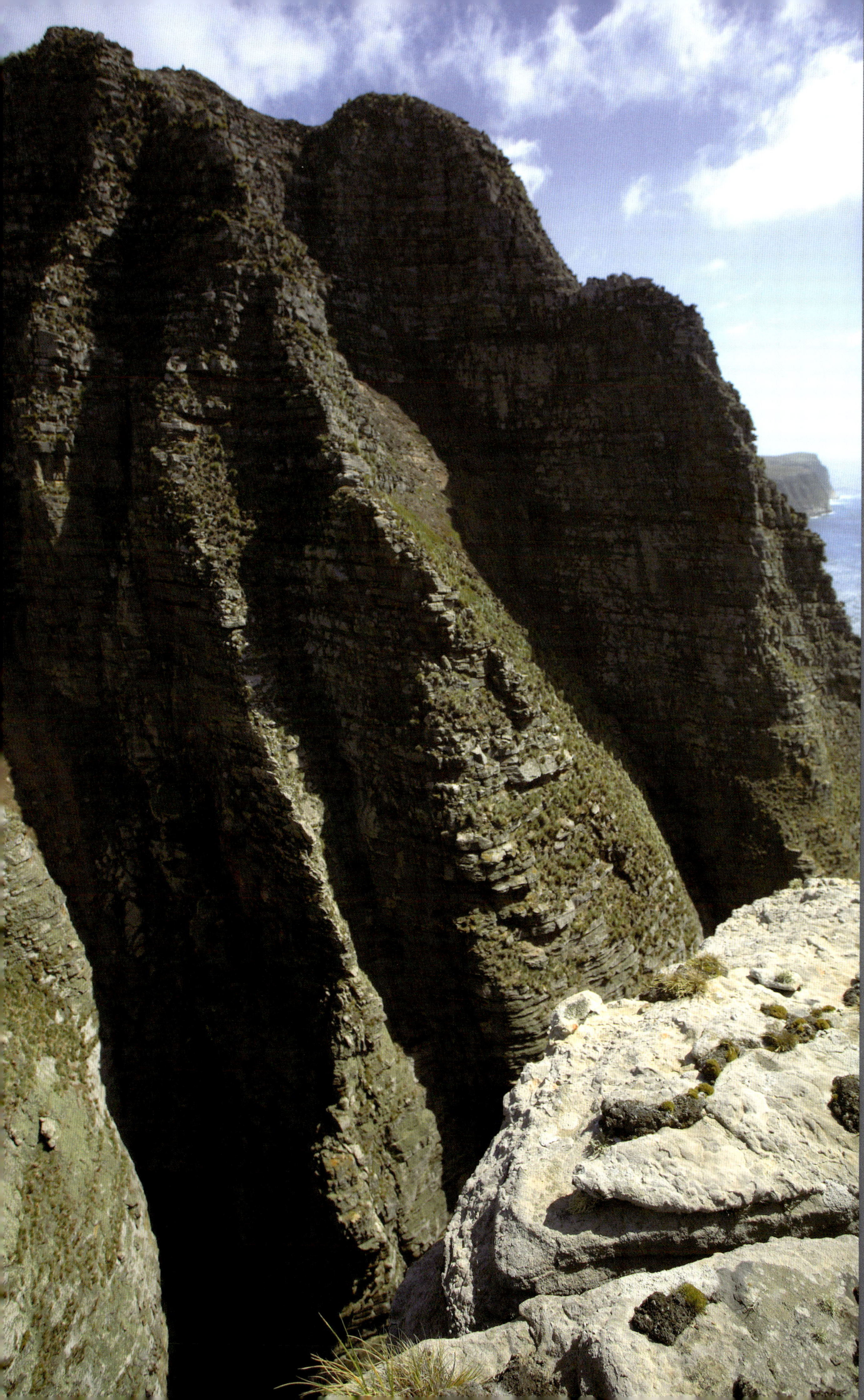

Marine Geology

The deeply indented coastline of the Falklands represents a drowned topography of river valleys incised when sea levels were relatively much lower than they are now. Marine erosion levels which may exist below present sea levels are difficult to investigate for obvious reasons. However, New Island was fortunate to have a team of divers who investigated the sub-littoral on the west coast of the island. They discovered that many areas were deeply undercut below the surface, apparently formed by wave action when sea levels were lower. These undercut areas were associated with accumulations of boulders which sloped down into deeper water and were presumed to be original beach deposits.

Caves and Gulches

There are several caves on the west side of the island. One of these does appear to traverse the western point of Landsend Bluff, the main mouth of this cave being on the west side cliffs and running through to a form of blow hole in the region of the Fur seal colony on the north east facing coast. Only one cave is easily accessible from the land. This lies at the southern end of the South End Tussac and is entered by scaling down a deep gulch and following the shore line to the south.

One or two gulches situated on the exposed western coast *(photo below)* are interesting examples illustrating how surface currents, originating from the most southern points of South America, flow in an easterly direction to eventually hit the shores of places like New Island. Large amounts of debris, especially Southern Beech *Nothofagus sp.*, often as complete trees with roots, are found in these gulches, quite likely having originated from the southern coastal regions of Chile and Straits of Magellan which support forests of this species. Pieces of *Nothofagus* with the characteristic teeth marks of Beaver *Castor canadensis* are also found. Canadian Beavers were introduced to Tierra del Fuego in 1944 where they have thrived.

Photo above: A view over The Rabbit's Ears, at the north eastern tip of New Island, looking towards Saddle and North islands. This bay collects large amounts of driftwood originating from the South American continent

The finding of a flint spearhead on one of the coastal points of New Island, also raises the hypothetical question as to whether New Island was an accidental or intentional landfall for Fuegian canoe indians at some point in the past. Their possible landing may well have resulted from these surface currents.

Peat and Soil

Soil layers on New Island are generally thin and with the very low rainfalls experienced on the island, vegetation and the subsequent formation of soils and peat is also low. Formations of peat do exist on New Island but are confined to very small, relatively shallow deposits. Although used by early settlers as a fuel, the quality was considered poor.

The only notable peat formations are those that exist in the valley which runs from the Settlement Rookery on the west coast, to the Settlement Harbour on the east side of the island. In this area the peat has been formed from Tussac grass, locally termed "bible" peat. Unlike many peat formations, annual accumulations of leaf debris remain intact as horizontal layers and can be separated like the leaves of a bible or book. Developing as a mat layer, which is often rich in total nitrogen, but poor in available nitrogen, it remains sour, often acidic, preventing breakdown by bacterial action. Unlike the peat formed in areas of much higher rainfall, it has not formed into the typical black "plastic" amorphous carbonaceous mass of the peat found in other areas of the Falklands. It lacks consolidation, remaining turf-like, light in colour and weight.

Hydrogeology and Water Resources

Water supplies on New Island are presently taken from natural springs, although in the past small streams were used as sources. The porosity of the bedrock formations, according to Aldiss & Edwards, can be expected to be low, although joints and fractures are usually well developed. These together with the weathered dolerite dykes could be forming effective aquicludes, fine grained layers of silt or clay, which absorb water and allow the release of sufficient amounts for the springs on the island.

At the present time, water supplies can be described as fair to moderate in terms of water drawn for domestic purposes. However, this has not always been the case and in a period prior to 1972 and for some ten years following, water supplies were very low. Quite probably over the 200 years or so that the island has been subjected to human activities, supplies have changed. There are no records of rainfall for New Island prior to 1995, so it is impossible to say how rainfall may have influenced supplies during the last 200 years. What is clear is that changes in land use have greatly influenced water supplies.

Personal communications with individuals who lived on New Island in the 1940s through to the 1960s do confirm that water supplies to the present settlement were not good. It was common practice for all buildings to have water tanks for collecting rainwater from their roofs. Some springs were piped but this was dependent on the form of pipe available. Probably not until the 1960s was cheaper alkathene pipe brought into the Falklands, making it financially and practically possible to tap sources from further afield.

As mentioned elsewhere, when the New Island Preservation Company first took over New Island, it was grossly overgrazed. Large areas were devoid of any vegetation *(example photo below)* and moving top soil was a common feature. Evaporation levels, although they could not be measured, must have been very high.

One or two water sources, notably one in Ship Harbour and one to the south of South Hill, ran throughout the year. Many others, especially in the area of the Settlement, ran dry in the summer. Water shortages became a very serious problem. In the summer of 1974, serious consideration was given to vacating the island due to the lack of water. Without vegetation to arrest rainfalls, now recorded as being one of the lowest in the Islands, run-offs took large amounts of rain directly to the coast and surface water quickly evaporated.

Following the removal of sheep and other livestock from New Island South in 1975, the vegetation rapidly improved and by 1982 there was a noticeable difference in many of the water sources. Springs that had previously dried up in mid summer continued to run indicating that water table levels were rising.

Water Supplies - Pre 1900

Historically, New Island was known to have been quite an important "watering" place for early American whaling vessels. There is written evidence from log books that water was taken from three sources: one or possibly two streams in Ship Harbour and in the Settlement Harbour, and one in South Harbour. None of the log book entries mention supplies being short or unavailable, so one concludes that water was plentiful in all months of the year for the period through the late 1700s and the mid 1800s.

Details on water supplies are not documented for the early period of settlement on New Island. It is known that at a point between 1883 and 1919 when Edward Nilsson was operating the island, in a notice to shipping, he was offering supplies of good water. In late December 1905 when the whale factory ship *Admiralen* operated from New Island, reference is made to the building of a water reservoir to obtain fresh water for the cooking boilers. The remains of such a reservoir still exist at the site in South Harbour.

Later, when the Salvesen whaling station was established in South Harbour, water would have been an important pre-requisite for such an operation. All the machinery was steam driven and with a workforce of 80-100 men, a good supply would have been needed.

At some point, underground clay pipe lines were laid from higher areas close to the station to increase water supplies *(see photo above right)*. The building of a hillside reservoir and a pumping station which brought water from the main pond at the South End Beach, are all indicators that water supplies were becoming short and may have been declining at that time.

Sheep and cattle farming had begun about 50 years earlier and would most probably

Photo above: Sections of clay piping used for water supplies to the whaling station (background: the remains of a steam-driven boiler)

by this time have had a significant effect on the island's vegetation. This in turn could have been having an impact on water tables and reducing supplies from springs.

Water Supplies Today

Available meteorological data for New Island does not show if weather patterns are changing, or if rainfall has increased in the last ten years. What is clear is that water sources in the period 2001 to 2006 appear to be stable and the island does not experience the serious water shortages of the 1970s. Measurements taken in the summers of 2001 to 2006 at the Prion Paddock spring indicate that this main source flows fairly consistently at the rate of 0.5 to 1 gallon per minute.

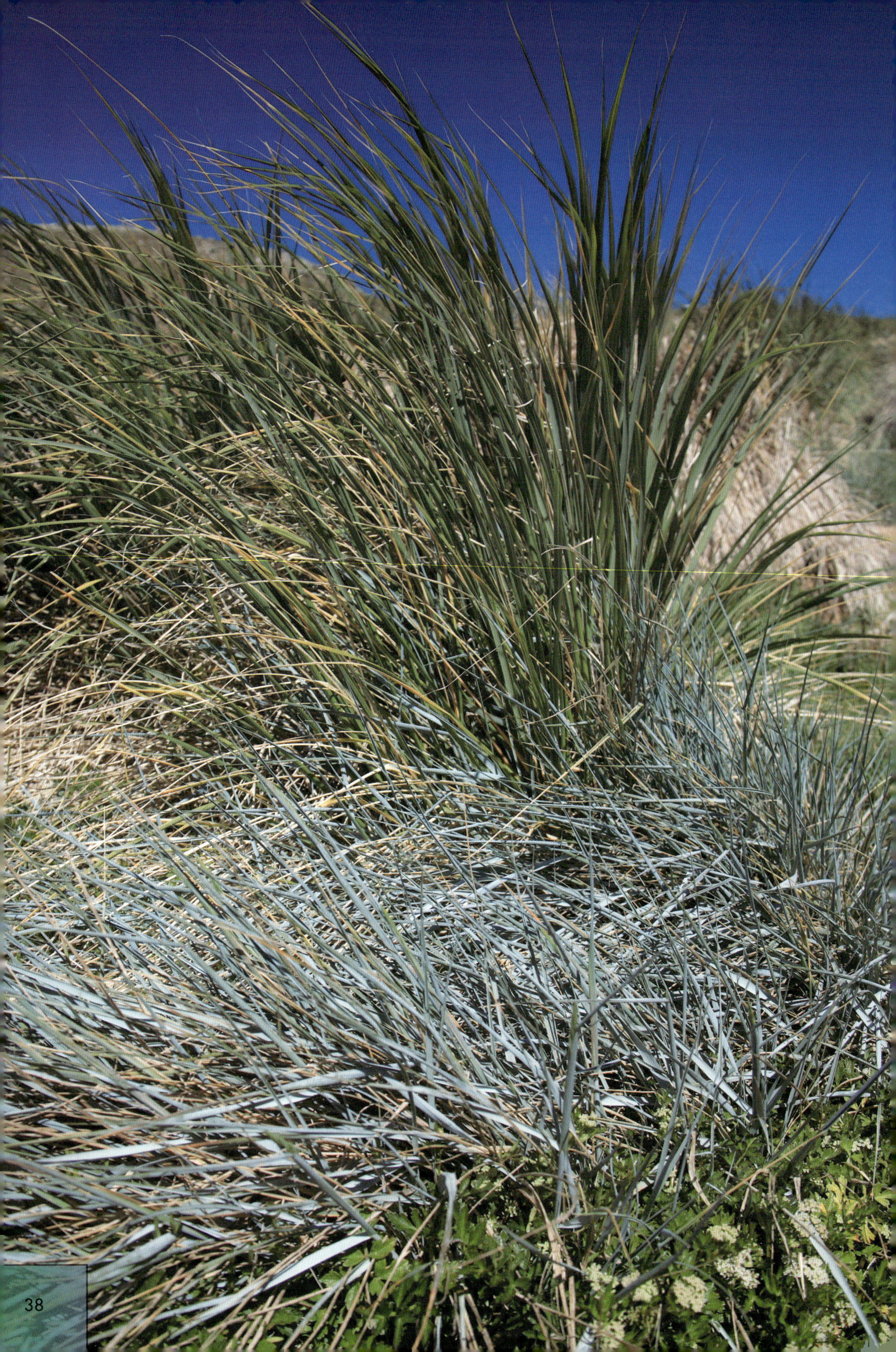

Marine & Terrestrial Vegetation

New Island presents an interesting example of the re-establishment of native vegetation following the removal of stock. The island will probably never revert to its original pristine state, due to the dominance in parts of introduced grasses, but as a model for the study of re-vegetation it is perhaps unique. For marine species, the island's extensive coastal environment provides a wide range of habitats for many kelps and algaes.

The first recorded visit by a botanist to New Island to make a collection of plants was that of American G.H. Snyder in December 1852. Swedish botanist Carl Skottsberg of the Swedish Magellanic Expedition visited the island in 1908. Between 1937 and 1938, botanist and pasture improvement specialist William Davies travelled to New Island to make recommendations for improving sheep grazing pastures.

Fairly detailed studies of the flora of New Island South have been made and a herbarium has been established (Vessal, Schenk & Strange, unpubl. data, 1996). Surveys were carried out using the Braun-Blanquet methodology and were aimed at covering different formations at varying elevations. The 1995 surveys positively identified 59 species. A number of plants, in particular grasses and sedges, have yet to be identified.
In December 1990 Prof. Almut Gerhardt made a collection of hepatics and mosses from the island (these works did not cover the former New Island North area). The description that follows is a tentative rough sketch of the island's vegetation.

Grassland

The Introduction of Yorkshire Fog
Much of the lower lying ground on the east part of the island is covered by grassland, in many places dominated by the introduced Yorkshire Fog *Holcus lanatus*, once favoured by stock farmers. This grass was extensively sown on New Island by J. J. Davis between 1949 and 1970, by aerial distribution using a Falkland Islands Government Air Service float plane. The main growth of this grass today is still reflected in areas where it was safe for such an aircraft to fly.

Where this grass is not heavily grazed by stock, as is the case on New Island now, it will often die back naturally, but it can also be attacked by the larvae of *Malvinius compressiventris*, one of the 23 species of weevil found in the Islands. In some areas the grass shows natural die-back, and in others the dead grass forms dense mats which when peeled back reveal the larvae of this weevil.

Other introduced grasses are present, such as Cocksfoot and Perennial Rye Grass. Short grassland is more often found at medium to high altitudes, particularly on some of the slopes of South Hill, where there is evidence of grazing by rabbits, but the distribution of introduced grasses, as mentioned above, may be an influence on their feeding.

Tussac Grass
According to historical descriptions, (e.g. Barnard, 1829) Tussac grass *Parodiochloa flabellata* formations once covered larger areas of New Island than it does today, but it was not extensive and was restricted to a few specific areas. Tussac is usually confined to coastal areas, generally within a radius of 300-400m of a shoreline, but at varying altitudes.

Photo opposite: Tussac grass, Blue Couch-grass and Wild Celery

Considerable areas were burnt ("Log of the *Aurora*", 1820, from a collection at The Nantucket Historical Association). These earlier burnt areas are identifiable today by layers of bright brick-red soils, below layers of later soil accumulations.

Overgrazing following the introduction of stock in the mid to late 1850s, was also responsible for Tussac loss. Although in some places this grass can grow to 3-4m, on New Island it rarely exceeds 2m, due to low rainfall. Since the removal of stock, Tussac is re-generating in many areas. Examples of this can be found on the summits of Cliff Peak, Precipice Hill and Cathedral Cliffs, at elevations of over 500 feet.

Other Native Grasses and Flowering Plants

Locally, other tall and robust native grasses can be found. These form dense, generally monospecific mats, the most important of which is Cinnamon Grass *Hierochloe redolens*, and Spiky grass *Poa robusta*. Since the removal of sheep, Cinnamon grass has expanded greatly to become a very common and important habitat for ground-nesting species. In December when it seeds it becomes an important source of feed for Black-chinned Siskins *(photo, below right)*.

Photo above: An example of the brick-red ground which can be seen where the earth has previously been exposed to intense fire

now dominant in moister areas is the Marsh Daisy *Aster vahlii*, and Pratia *Pratia repens*. Wild Celery *Apium australe*, Lady's Slipper *Calceolaria fothergillii* and Scurvy Grass *Oxalis enneaphylla* are now common.

Re-vegetation of Eroded Areas

Sheep's Sorrel *Rumex acetosella* is mostly found on eroded peat or open soil, on areas that have been disturbed, noticeably by Prion excavation activities. Areas exposed to high levels of nitrates from bird guano, such as Prion and Gentoo penguin breeding sites, are often dominated by the annual Groundsel *Senecio vulgaris*.

In some areas other native species occur and are increasing, for example, the Mountain Blue grass *Poa alopecurus* and the Blue Couch-grass *Agropyron magellanicum*. Small stands of the uncommon Sword Grass *Carex trifida* also grow on the island, but this species is rare.

A plant recorded as rare to uncommon before the removal of sheep and

Photo left: Tussac grass continues to re-vegetate areas where livestock had once caused widespread erosion

Heath Formation

Large sections of the low and mid-altitude ground are covered by heath formation. This is dominated by the dwarf shrub Diddle-dee *Empetrum rubrum*, and locally by the Mountain Berry *Pernettya pumila*. Growing in areas usually dominated by Diddle-dee, there are pure beds of Fern *Blechnum sp*. One of the most common of these is *Blechnum penna-marina* forming monospecific carpets. This fern is rapidly replacing die-back areas once dominated by Yorkshire Fog.

Cushion Plants

Cushion plants are the dominant feldmark formations, growing in more exposed situations on higher ground and ridges. Common species include the Balsam Bog *Bolax gummifera*, different *Azorella* species and *Nassauvia gaudichaudii*.

Since the removal of sheep, the re-establishment of these plant forms has been one of the most noticeable changes in the island's vegetation. Although Balsam is more common today, the island still lacks the large cushion-like formations which can be seen, for example, on neighbouring North Island, which has never been subjected to sheep and cattle grazing.

Native Boxwood

Native Boxwood *Hebe elliptica* grows in some coastal areas of New Island, in particular around the settlement. In its native habitat it is restricted to West Falkland, especially on a small group of selected islands. Since the removal of stock, this slow growing, woody evergreen shrub is regenerating on the island. Examples of a hybrid Boxwood exists on New Island. Formed from the Falklands native Boxwood and a species native to New Zealand, it bears the name *Hebe francisciana*.

Photo above: The hybrid Boxwood, Hebe francisciana

Flora Conservation

A relatively high proportion of the native Falkland Islands' flora is of conservation concern, and a number of species are endemic to the islands (D.M. Moore 1967; Broughton & McAdam 2002). The introduction of sheep, and to some extent cattle, to New Island had two major effects:

- Vegetation became heavily grazed resulting in a number of plant species either disappearing or being much reduced. As a result of de-vegetation, evaporation levels would have risen making the surface of the island drier.

- The second major effect to the island's surface layers and some plants, was the compacting of soil layers caused by the cloven feet of sheep. Plants such as Balsam Bog *Bolax gummifera* are easily destroyed by a cloven hoof breaking through the surface of its cushion and causing the plant to rot.

New Island, being one of few medium-sized islands from which stock has been removed, may present good opportunities for the conservation of species sensitive to grazing.

Further work is necessary to identify species and populations that have appeared since the previous survey, carried out in 1995, in order to show their development since the removal of grazers. Surveys of the recently acquired northern end of the island are also necessary.

Photos above & left: A comparison between the vegetation in Rookery valley, 1979 (above) and 2007 (left). An area once heavily grazed by livestock, it now supports dense Blue Couch-grass, Spiky grass, Tussac and many species of bird

Photos above, from left: Pratia in flower, Fern (Blechnum sp.) and the marine algae Durvillea antarctica

Marine Species

Kelp and Marine Algae

In broad terms the sub littoral might be classed into two main zones: one which fringes deep water along the western coast of the island; and one which forms along the shallower waters on the lee shore facing east. These two areas can then be divided into three zones as follows:

Offshore in depths of 4-30m (13-98ft) is a zone supporting the Giant Kelp *Macrocystis pyrifera* and Tree Kelp *Lessonia flavicans,* two very common species which form dense beds around the island, but in particular on the eastern coasts.

From the extreme low water mark and extending out to 3-4m (9-13ft) in depth is a fringe zone. This area supports two species of Tree Kelp *Lessonia frutescens* and *Lessonia nigrescens.* Also growing in this zone are two large species of marine algae, *Durvillea antarctica* and *Durvillea caepestipes (shown in photo, below, with Sea Lions).*

The third zone lies in the inter-tidal areas; the middle shore between the average low and high water marks. On New Island two small species of marine algae are common; a species of Sea Lettuce *Ulva sp.* which is a common feed for Kelp Geese, and a species of *Iridaea* which is also grazed by geese.

Very few studies have been made of New Island's inshore marine environment and many other species of marine algae require identification.

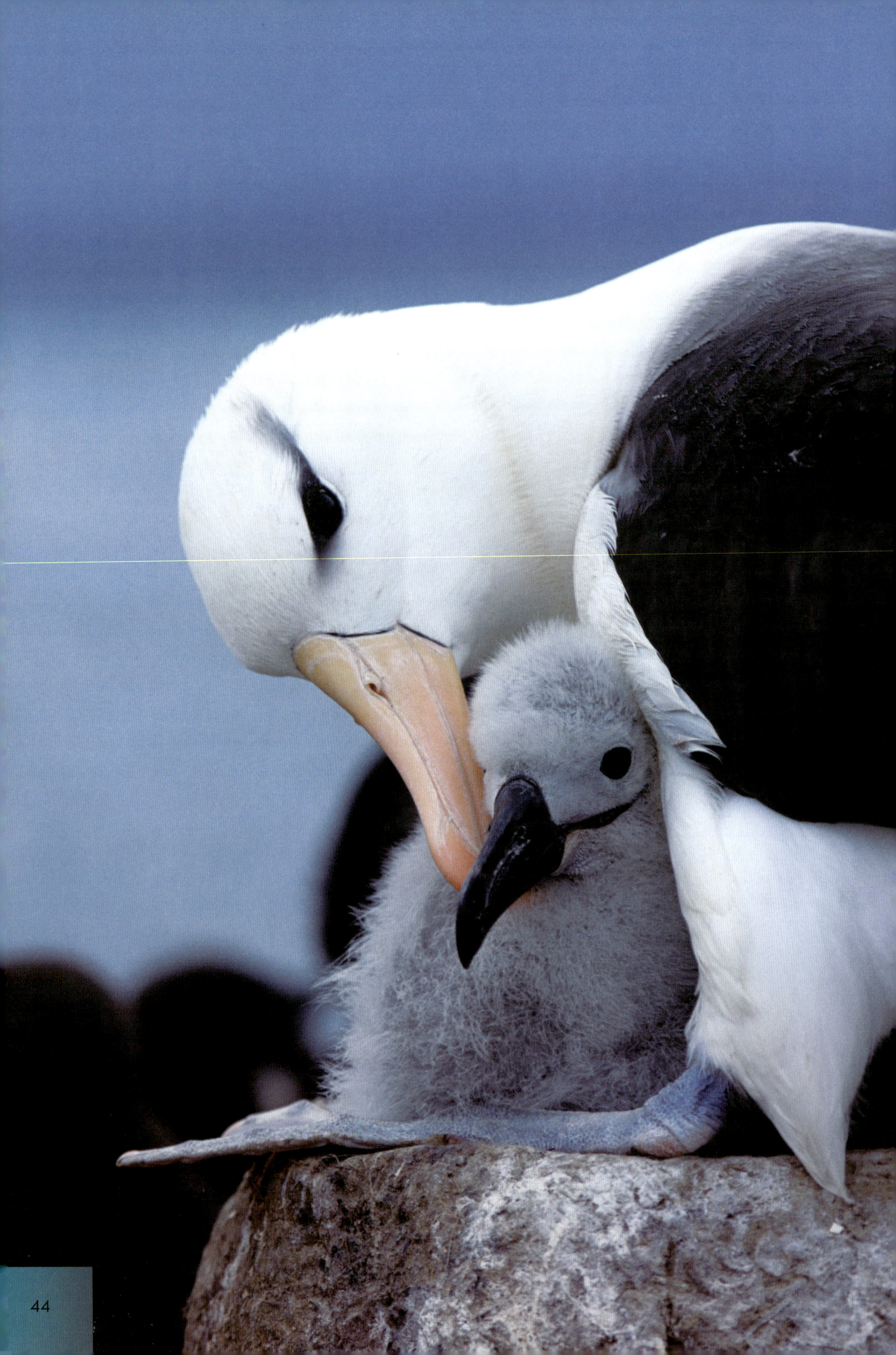

Birds

New Island has 39 regularly breeding species of bird; 65% of the total breeding species found in the Falkland Islands. Seabirds make up the largest numbers, followed by geese, passerines, birds of prey and shorebirds.
This section gives a brief introduction to each of these breeding species, including further information regarding population, distribution and research details, where available.

The information that follows is based on surveys, counts and observations or field research, carried out on the New Island South area of the reserve only, (unless otherwise stated). However, it can be noted that in general, both the North and the South parts of the island are very comparable in terms of species.

Although recorded but not as breeding, it is possible the island holds small numbers of species such as Wilson's Storm Petrel, Dove Prion, and Diving Petrel. The latter species is known to breed on New Island's offshore property, Seal Rocks.

Significant populations of several globally threatened or endangered species breeding on New Island give the reserve its Important Bird Area (IBA) status. These particular species are highlighted in boxes for easy reference, and include their Red List Status (International Union for the Conservation of Nature and Natural Resources) as correct at the time of publishing (March 2007).

Further information relevant to this section can be found in Annexes 4, 5 & 6, and a map of New Island, showing areas mentioned in the following pages, can be viewed on page 151.

Penguins

Magellanic Penguin *Spheniscus magellanicus*
IUCN Red List Status: Near Threatened

Magellanic penguins are migratory birds that winter north of the Falkland Islands, along the Patagonian Shelf. They feed mostly on squid and fish.
They are widespread as nesting birds on New Island South, but being burrow nesters, they are relatively difficult to count and study.

Census Work
Two censuses have been made of the population on New Island South. The first was carried out as a trial to establish a suitable method. This took place in late February 1999 (C. S. & T. C. Lamey) and counted groups of moulting birds which tend to form around breeding areas. The total counted was 600 birds. However, it should be noted that this census ignored individuals that were known to be moulting in burrows and was also restricted to an area from the Settlement to the north end of the airstrip.

Between 27 January and 8 February 2001 a more thorough survey was conducted of both breeding pairs and chicks on New Island South (A. van Buren & J. Sigman). This census revealed 3,724 adult pairs and 573 chicks.

Photo opposite: Black-browed Albatross and chick

Gentoo Penguin *Pygoscelis papua*
IUCN Red List Status: Near Threatened

Gentoo penguins are relatively sedentary birds, feeding mostly on lobster krill, fish and squid in West Falkland.

On New Island there are two main areas where colonies of breeding Gentoo Penguins can be found: one at the North end of the island, and one at the South end. Numbers have varied historically as a result of different attitudes towards them, varying from exploitation and persecution in the past, to the protection that they have today.

In 1933, Government naturalist, A.G. Bennett counted 2,500 Gentoo nests on New Island. When Ian Strange purchased the island in 1972, numbers were in the low hundreds. From thereon, numbers steadily increased.

The table below shows how numbers on New Island South fluctuated over the subsequent years (*numbers were obtained by counting incubating birds in the first or second week of November*):

Year	Number of breeding pairs (New Island South reserve)
1986	2,782
1999	1,234
2001	2,485[A]
2002	0[B]
2003	534
2004	375
2005	437
2006	560

[A] - In this breeding season, the North end colonies were estimated to hold approximately 5,000 pairs (T. Chater, pers. comm.).

[B] - In the breeding season of 2002, a massive seabird mortality, apparently caused by a harmful algal bloom, resulted in total breeding failure, adult mortality and possibly emigration. A similar level of destruction affected the North end colonies.

The following season of 2003 saw 534 nesting pairs: only 21% of the original South reserve breeding population of the 2001 season.

Further low level mortality took place in the summer of 2003, further reducing the numbers of breeding Gentoos in the following season.

King Penguin *Aptenodytes patagonica*
The Falkland Islands is the most northerly point of this species' range, with relatively few breeding sites in the Islands.
On New Island King Penguins have been recorded breeding in very small numbers amongst Gentoo penguins at the northern end of the island since the mid 1960's, and perhaps even earlier. Individual birds are sometimes found with Gentoos at the southern colony sites of this species, but not recorded as breeding.

*Photo above: Part of the North End Gentoo colony as it was in 1973;
Photo right: Part of the same colony in 2006 (shown from the opposite side of the valley).
Gentoo numbers on New Island are just a fraction of what they used to be, but the population appears to be slowly recovering.*

Rockhopper Penguin *Eudyptes chrysocome*
IUCN Red List Status: Vulnerable

Rockhopper penguins are long-distance migrants that are absent from New Island between March and October. They feed mostly on small squid and pelagic crustaceans.
On New Island they nest in four localities, the largest colony being the Settlement Rookery. Rockhopper penguins have suffered a dramatic population decline in the Falklands during the 20th century. Such decline seems to be continuing and has been clearly felt on New Island where present numbers are just a small fraction of what they used to be.

Census Work

Due to logistical difficulties in counting, no detailed censuses of the whole colony have been possible in the past. Estimates made of the Settlement Rookery in the mid- to late 1970s gave figures of 30-40,000 pairs (I.J Strange, pers. obs.). Between 11 and 26 October 2001 a census was carried out of adults returning to a section of the main Settlement Colony known as "The Bowl". This census used new technology employing infra-red sensors, coupled to an electronic counter. Male birds are the first to return to the colony and were counted, followed by the females. The two counts gave very comparable figures, with a total breeding population for this isolated section of the Settlement Colony of 2,593 pairs. The Bowl was estimated to contain approximately one quarter of the total Settlement Colony population ("Counting Rockhopper Penguins Electronically", Strange, 2001, NISCT Report).

Standardised whole-day counts of Rockhoppers coming ashore on selected days in early December (11-13 Dec, at the brooding stage when the male parent remains at the nest and thus, only one adult per pair is counted), have resulted in the following figures for for penguins arriving at the Settlement colony:

- 2003:   6,683
- 2004:   5,142
- 2005:   4,411
- 2006:   5,687

These numbers above have been shown to be highly correlated with estimates of actual breeding pairs (Catry et al., 2005). More research is needed to assess the repeatability of such counts and derived estimates. On New Island, large numbers of Rockhoppers nest in dense stands of Tussac, where nest counts are not practical.

Research

The causes of the Rockhopper penguin population decline are unknown, but the fact that this decline occurred at all breeding sites in the Falklands suggests that it is linked to oceanographic changes.

Recent research on New Island concluded that there are no important land-based negative factors affecting the reproduction of the species, and that Rockhopper penguins are only rarely predated by introduced mammals (Matias 2005, Matias & Catry, unpublished).

A detailed study following the complete breeding cycle of Rockhopper penguins was started in 2006 by Maud Poisbleau with assistance from Laurent Demongin *(photo, right)*, with funding by the Deutsche Forschungsgemeinschaft, Germany, assured until at least 2011. This will use new technologies for automated monitoring. Starting in the 2006 season, unique PIT tags (transponders) have been used to mark Rockhopper penguins at New Island. Because penguins walk to their colonies, transponders enable the setup of an automated monitoring system. This will consist of an infrared beam and an antenna to read transponders, situated at a weighbridge. This detailed data on attendance and body condition of marked individuals will contribute to understanding how oceanographic conditions affect this species.

Satellite Tracking of Rockhopper Penguins

A program involving the satellite tracking of Rockhopper penguins was carried out in the years 1997 to 2004. This looked at the foraging trips carried out by breeding birds from the Settlement Rookery. This showed the importance of the Special Co-Operation Area (licensed for future oil exploration) as a major feeding area for Rockhoppers during the breeding season, and that some birds made trips almost as far as the mainland of South America (Boersma et al. 2002).

The possibility that a portion of the Falklands' population of Rockhopper penguins could have re-located to areas such as Isla Noir, Chile, where numbers are increasing, should be considered as a possible factor in the decline of this species on New Island (W. Scott Drieschman, pers. comm.).

Albatrosses, Petrels and Shearwaters

Black-browed Albatross *Thalassarche melanophrys*
IUCN Red List Status: Endangered

The Falkland Islands host the majority of the world population of this widespread species. New Island, despite being a secondary colony within the Falklands, still holds numbers of this species that are significant in global terms.

Census Work

Numbers of Black-browed albatross have shown a long-term increase at the Settlement Rookery since 1977 (see Graph 1, below), when 998 pairs were recorded. A count of the same area in 2006 gave a total of 2,001 pairs, showing that the breeding population of these birds in this area has more than doubled over the 29 year period.

Overall combined aerial and ground surveys of New Island South, including Landsend Bluff, have also shown a continuous population increase over these years. On 20 October 2000, a census yielded 4,454 occupied nests. On 29 September 2004 the total was 5,214. An aerial survey of the same areas on 27 September 2006 gave a total of 6,324, showing an increase of approximately 9% per annum over the last two years.

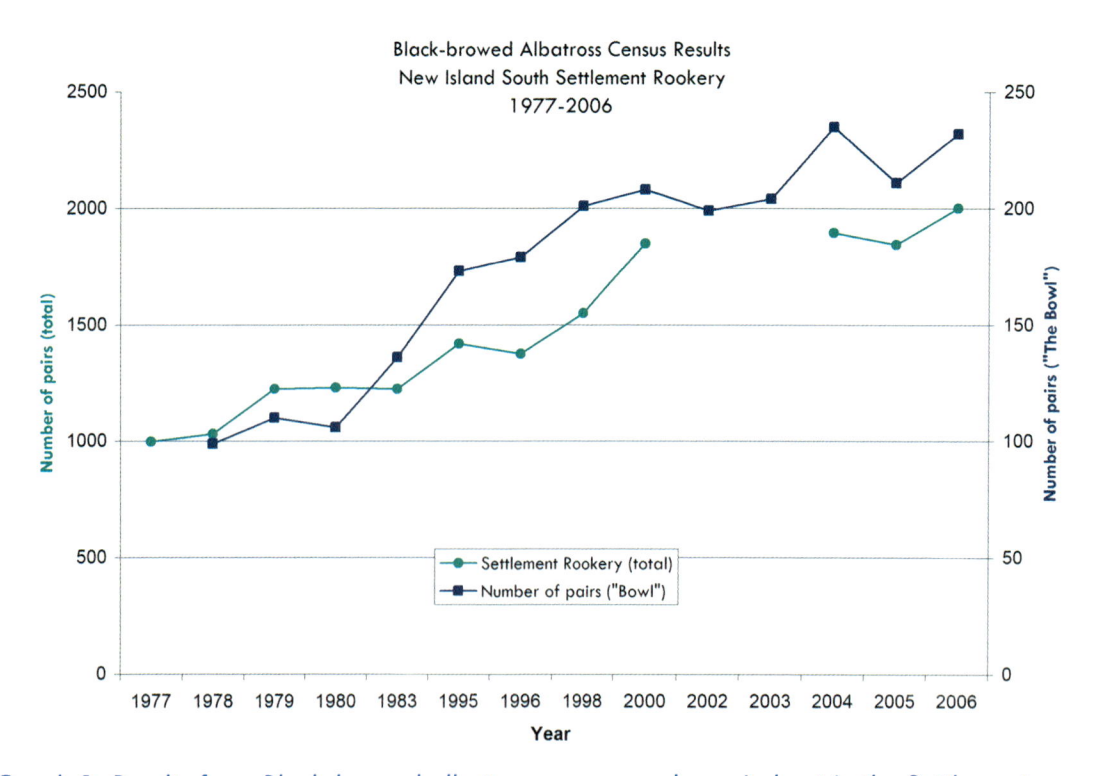

Graph 1: Results from Black-browed albatross census work carried out in the Settlement Rookery of New Island South, between 1977 and 2006; and from an isolated section of the rookery known as "The Bowl", between 1978 and 2006. Surveys carried out by Ian J. Strange, combining aerial photography and ground survey methods.
(NB: Data for the Settlement Rookery total in the years 2002 and 2003 was not collected).

Photos: Examples of the type of terrain on which Black-browed albatross nest on New Island south (West cliff colonies), and an example of the quality of image that can be obtained through aerial photography for counting numbers of these birds.

The results obtained from these censuses are consistent with results obtained from aerial surveys of other Black-browed albatross colonies in the Falkland Islands (I.J. Strange unpubl. data. For more details, see Annex 5).

The factors underlying this population growth in some areas of the Falklands are unknown, but detailed research is currently being conducted on New Island, and data collected may assist in explaining these findings (see following pages).

Research

In the breeding season of 2003, Dr Paulo Catry started a detailed population dynamics and breeding ecology study of Black-browed albatross on the reserve. With its fourth year now complete, this study is monitoring the breeding success and survival of over 600 albatrosses on an annual basis, and in the 2006 season, 300 albatross chicks (in the late stages of their development) were also banded for future monitoring.

At the same time, a range of behavioural studies are being conducted, including comparative studies with albatross nesting on Bird Island, South Georgia (in partnership with the British Antarctic Survey, and also with the support of individual researchers, namely Rafael Matias and Miguel Lecoq).

In collaboration with Orea Anderson and Stuart Bearhop (Queen's University, Belfast) a study on the feeding specializations of individual albatross is also being carried out, to try to evaluate if some birds are more at risk from accidental mortality in fishing gear than others. Data collected from past studies on New Island suggest that albatross nesting on the reserve rely heavily on fish offal and discards from fishing vessels (K. Thompson & P. Catry, unpubl. data), which may be a reason for their increase, despite their vulnerability when associating with long-line fishing vessels.

Funding for the continuation of these studies by Dr Paulo Catry has been secured until 2010, thanks to the Portuguese Science Foundation and the Falkland Islands Government.

Photo above: A Black-browed albatross nest-building with mud
Above left: A pair of albatross engaged in courtship on the cliff's edge

Thin-billed Prion *Pachyptila belcheri*

New Island hosts the largest breeding colony of this species in the world. Prions breed all over the island, from hill tops to sea level, but they seem to prefer steeper ground (excluding cliffs) covered by various species of grasses; however, they also nest in flat areas and in most vegetation formations found on the island.

Census Work

A relatively detailed survey was carried out in 2001/02, giving an estimated 1,081,000 apparently active nest burrow entrances on New Island South (95% confidence limits 815,000 – 1,346,000) (Catry et al. 2003). Similar numbers probably occur on the north side of the island, but a survey is needed in order to establish populations on that part of the island.

More research is needed to assess the correspondence of nest burrow entrances to breeding pairs. Recent work using a burrow scope suggests that on the higher ground, the assumption that one burrow entrance corresponds, on average, to one breeding pair, is over-optimistic. However, the situation is probably different at lower levels, where deep soil allows prions to excavate complex networks with numerous ramifications; unfortunately, here burrows are too deep to be effectively explored using a burrow scope.

Research

On New Island, Thin-billed prions have been the subject of detailed behavioural (Monica Silva, 1998-2001) (Quillfeldt et al. 2006) and ecological long-term studies, (Quillfeldt et al. 2003, 2007) which continue today.

Monitoring has used consistent methodology since 2003, and has established a strong relationship between sea surface temperatures and provisioning frequencies (Quillfeldt et al. 2007).

Thin-billed prions attend their chicks at night; the absence of adults from the nest burrow during the day provides the opportunity to collect data on chick provisioning with very little disturbance to the birds.

Thin-billed prions feed on the same type of prey that most of the commercially targeted squid and fish prey on, on small crustaceans such as euphausids and amphipods. Prions are thus potentially suitable for assessing amphipod and euphausid abundance. They have flexible foraging strategies, using short foraging trips as well as long trips of up to 8 days (Quillfeldt et al. in press), and measures of feeding rates can thus serve as a real-time monitor of food availability.

Funding for the continuation of the monitoring programme by Dr Petra Quillfeldt on New Island has been obtained from the Deutsche Forschungsgemeinschaft, Germany until at least 2011 (Emmy Noether Programme, Grant Qu148-1ff).

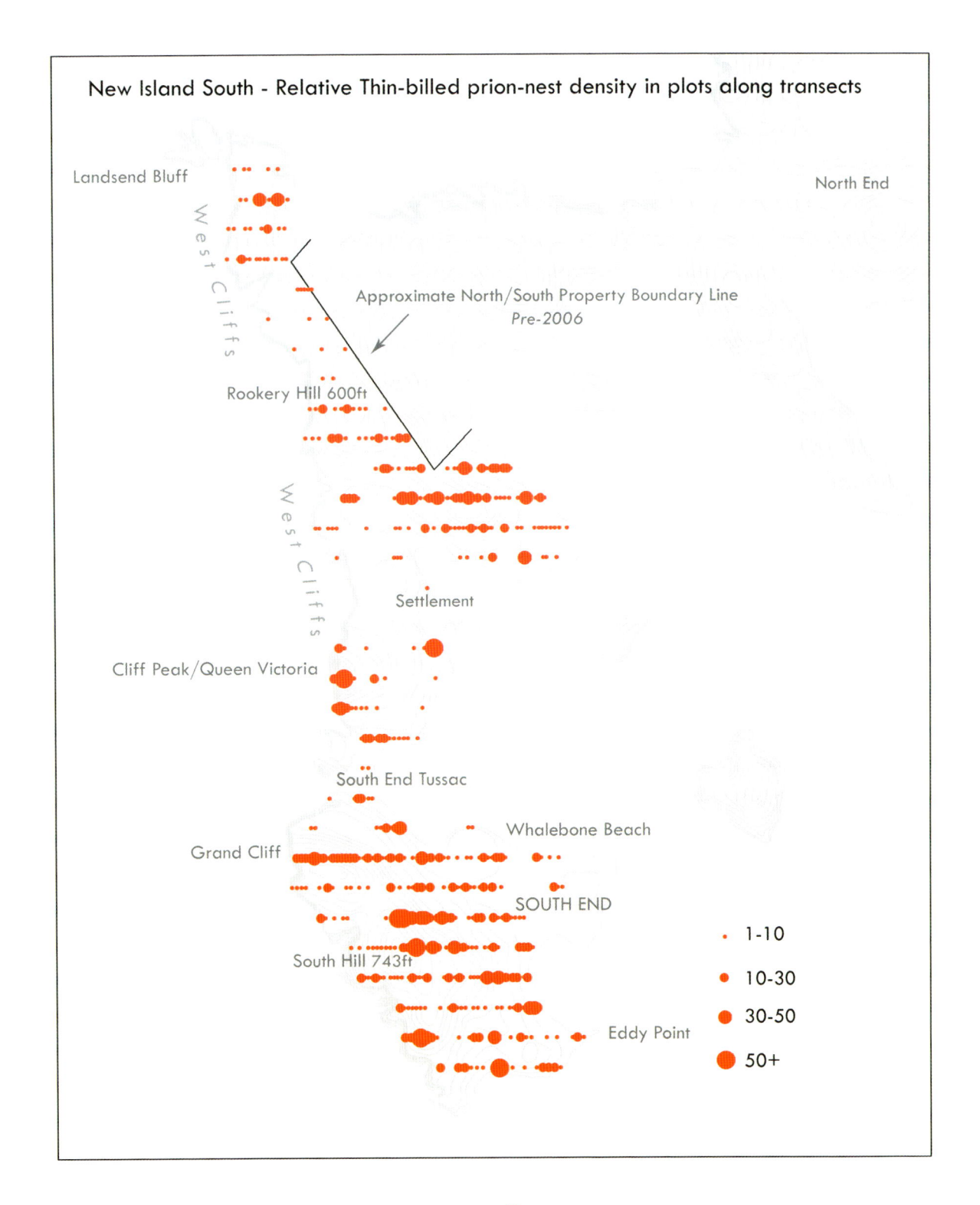

New Island South - Relative Thin-billed prion-nest density in plots along transects

Landsend Bluff — North End
West Cliffs
Approximate North/South Property Boundary Line Pre-2006
Rookery Hill 600ft
West Cliffs
Settlement
Cliff Peak/Queen Victoria
South End Tussac
Whalebone Beach
Grand Cliff
SOUTH END
South Hill 743ft
Eddy Point

- 1-10
- 10-30
- 30-50
- 50+

Above: Number of prion burrow entrances in 50m² plots on New Island South. Results from a survey carried out in January/February 2002, by Paulo Catry & Ana Campos. Redrawn from data published in Catry et al. (2003).

Photo opposite: Dr Petra Quillfeldt holding a Thin-billed prion chick, close to fledging, for measurements, as part of the current research being carried out on this species.

Giant Petrel *Macronectes giganteus*
IUCN Red List Status: Vulnerable

A species rapidly increasing in the Falkland Islands, the Giant Petrel is commonly seen around the coasts of New Island. A few pairs nested on Eddy Point in the 1970s, and a small colony of some 30-40 pairs nested in the area of The Rabbits Ears at the north eastern tip of the island in 2006.

White-chinned Petrel
Procellaria aequinoctialis

New Island hosts one of the very few White-chinned petrel colonies known to exist in the Falkland Islands. White-chinned petrels are known to be frequent victims of long-line fisheries and their populations are thought to be declining worldwide.

Breeding was first confirmed in 1972 when it was estimated that there were 30-32 occupied burrows. In December 1981 there were between 30 and 40 pairs, and in 2000 it was estimated that no more than 50 pairs occupied the site.
In the breeding season of 2004, 36 apparently occupied burrows were recorded (census carried out using playbacks), with the total population estimated at 40 pairs.
26 nests with eggs were recorded in 2005 (census carried out using a burrow scope [Reid & Catry 2006]).
There is no evidence of a long-term change in numbers nesting on New Island.

On New Island, the small colony is near the top of Rookery Hill. Nest burrows are situated in low banks of peat soil on an exposed hillside. These banks are subject to winter erosion, with some nest burrows collapsing in some years, which might be a limiting factor for the nesting population.

Sooty Shearwater *Puffinus griseus*
IUCN Red List Status: Near Threatened

Sooty shearwaters are common in Falkland Islands waters, but with very few breeding sites recorded in the Islands. They are burrow-nesters that only come ashore under the cover of night.

On New Island they nest in extremely small numbers on Rookery Hill, amongst prions and White-chinned petrels. In 1981 one pair was discovered occupying a burrow. In 2004 only one active nest was detected in this area during a White-chinned petrel survey, but a few more might have gone unnoticed. As far as it is known, Sooty shearwaters have always been very scarce on New Island.

Photo left: White-chinned Petrel, calling

Cormorants

Blue-eyed/King Cormorant
Phalacrocorax atriceps albiventer

On New Island, Blue-eyed Cormorants or Shags nest at three sites, but the majority are found in the main Settlement Rookery area.

Census Work

A special effort was directed at estimating the number of pairs of Blue-eyed Shags nesting in this main colony. For this, early in the breeding season of 2004, before old nests from the previous season were rebuilt, nest density was calculated in the main nesting colony. Measurements of the surface area of the main colony were then taken and the resulting estimate was 2930 nesting pairs of this species for 2003. Numbers for the 2004 season were similar.

In 2004 nests were also counted in other sub-colonies in mid-November. There were 367 nests in mixed colonies with Rockhopper penguins and/or albatross nests. This yields a total of 3,297 nests on New Island South in 2004 (it should be noted that this estimate includes a small number of nests where eggs were apparently not laid).
However, it should be noted that this methodology may slightly over-estimate the actual number of active nests, because nests are visible for several years after the last use.

Research

The foraging grounds of these birds seem to be mostly located towards the east of New Island. Opportunistic observations suggest that fish and lobster krill are important elements in their diet. A study on this species

Photo above: PhD student Riek van Noordwijk working with King Cormorants

commenced in the 2005 breeding season and will continue until 2009 (in the framework of the Emmy Noether Programme, Grant Qu148-1 to P. Quillfeldt).

From the 2006 field season, in addition to monitoring parameters of breeding success, the work on the species has included the use of time-depth and compass loggers in order to study the inter-relationships between foraging and the oceanographic conditions. This work will continue until at least 2009.

Rock Shag *Phalacrocorax magellanicus*

On New Island, Rock shags nest on small inaccessible colonies on the western cliffs, making their study and monitoring almost impossible without the use of a small boat.

Seven small colonies (varying in size from 4 to 20 nests) were located and mapped (seen from land) on New Island South.
Rock shags are also present in good numbers on the small islands surrounding New Island.

Photo above: Black-crowned Night Heron chicks

Herons

Black-crowned Night Heron
Nycticorax nycticorax
Night herons are fairly common along the eastern lee shore of New Island where they forage mostly along the seashore, taking small fish and other marine life. Night Herons are also known to prey on nestlings of Siskins, and individuals have been seen at night in areas of prion burrows, suggesting that they may also prey on this species.

On New Island South, they nest regularly inside the hull of the *Protector*, the old vessel stranded at the Settlement (6 active nests were recorded there in 2005).
In December 2006 a small breeding colony of 4 was found near Ship Harbour. It is likely that other small nest sites exist towards the southern end of the island, where birds in adult plumage are regularly seen.

Geese and Ducks

Ruddy-headed Goose
Chloephaga rubidiceps
Comparing New Island with breeding sites where this species is more common, it is most probable that the island is too dry for this goose. The species is also far less aggressive than the larger Upland goose, which is a factor to be considered.

Census Work
From the breeding season of 2003 to the 2005 season, no more than half a dozen pairs have attempted to nest on New Island South each year, most of these being unsuccessful.
Numbers of geese counted in December reached a maximum of 109 adult or sub-adult birds in 2005 (most of them moulting in Ship Harbour); maximum counts in 2003 and 2004 were 74 and 45 adult birds, respectively.
The recorded each year clearly show that some birds must be coming from other islands to moult on New Island.

Upland Goose
Chloephaga picta leucoptera
Upland geese are abundant, widespread and remarkably tame on New Island. Here, they benefit mainly from a lack of persecution.

Census Work
A detailed census made between 20-21 October 1996 when pairs with nests, goslings and territories held by adult males, (assumed with females on nests), gave a total of 156 pairs, 336 non-breeding females and 281 non-breeding males. This census only covered the South End area of New Island (from the old fence line on the south side of the South End Tussac area), excluding the settlement and area to the north.
An estimate, based on partial and whole-

Photo left: A female Upland goose with goslings

island counts of broods, nests and apparently failed breeders, suggests that from 2003 to 2005, between 200 and 400 Upland geese pairs nested annually on New Island South. A study of the effects of this high breeding density on population parameters has been initiated and will hopefully continue in the near future (Quillfeldt et al. 2005, Gladbach arcticle 2006 in Penguin News).

Counts made of moulting Upland geese on the South reserve in 2003, 2004 and 2005, (around 1st December) have resulted in 1,880, 1,538 and 1,140 individuals respectively.

The total number of moulting birds was slightly under-estimated, as on New Island some individuals only join moulting flocks during December (NB: these counts excluded flocking non-breeders that were not moulting).

The numbers recorded, their variation, and the fact that generally there is an obvious decline in numbers after the completion of moult, suggest that New Island might harbour moulting Upland geese that originate from other areas of the Falkland Islands. However, following moult, birds do tend to disperse more widely on the island, which may be a factor to consider.

The movement of young geese away from New Island has been shown with ringed birds. Two fledglings ringed in January 2006 were later recovered 35 miles away at Port Stephens on West Falkland in June 2006. Other fledglings ringed at the same time have remained close to their site of hatching.

Photo below: PhD student Anja Gladbach taking measurements of an Upland goose

Kelp Goose
Chloephaga hybrida malvinarum
Kelp geese are year-round residents on New Island, living mostly along the sheltered east coast where they graze on seaweed, in particular Sea Lettuce *Ulva sp.*

For at least a decade or more, a group of between 40 and 45 birds of mixed ages are almost continually resident on the Protector Beach in the Settlement.

Systematic counts along the east coast, plus occasional observations on the west cliffs, indicate that the total number of adult and sub-adult individuals present on New Island South, in the 2003 and 2004 summer seasons, was 110-120 individuals in each year.
Of these, only 24 were paired and territorial, most of which attempted to nest (see Catry & Campos 2004 and Catry et al. 2005 for more details).

Falkland Flightless Steamer Duck
Tachyeres brachydactyla

This is a flightless and resident species endemic to the Falkland Islands that lives almost permanently in the sea. Some small local movements must occur regularly, because numbers on New Island South vary within and between the breeding seasons (Catry & Campos 2004, Catry et al. 2005). On New Island, Steamer ducks are found mostly along the eastern, more sheltered coast.

Census Work
In November 1996 a coastal survey of New Island South, excluding the west cliff areas, gave a figure of 73 adult birds, of which 21 were pairs (Lea & Thalmann, 1996).

The numbers of apparently occupied territories (or territorial pairs), including those on the west coast, were 25-30 in 2003, 10-15 in 2004 and 14-17 in 2005.

On average less than half a dozen broods are successfully raised each year within the limits of the South reserve. This low number is partly compensated for by the fact that broods raised to fledging often include 5-7, and sometimes 8, ducklings and that the species is long-lived.

Patagonian Crested Duck
Lophonetta s. specularoides
On New Island, Crested duck can be regularly found on sheltered sea coasts and on the South End Pond. Numbers of this species fluctuate during spring and summer.

Generally, less than 10 broods can be seen on New Island South in any summer season (e.g. 7 in 2003 and 6 in 2005).
Adults and sub-adults counted during early December 2003, 2004 and 2005 numbered 69, 44 and 49, respectively.

Yellow-billed Teal
Anas flavirostris
The Yellow-billed teal is scarce as a breeding bird on New Island South, with only some 1-3 pairs known to have attempted breeding in each of the three most recent years.
Flocks of non-breeders originating from other parts of the Falklands can be found gathering at the South End Pond from mid-summer (e.g. 70 individuals on 1st February 2005).

Photo above: Yellow-billed Teal with ducklings

Raptors

Crested Caracara *Polyborus p. plancus*
In the summer seasons of 2003, 2004 and 2005, only one pair of this species was present on New Island South. In the first two years, pairs either did not nest, or were unsuccessful, but in 2005 one pair nested in one of the South End Tussac gulches and raised one fledgling.
In 2006, three territorial pairs of this caracara were counted on the South reserve and successful breeding was confirmed in two of these.

Peregrine Falcon *Falco peregrinus cassini*
Peregrines are known to nest in small numbers along the west cliffs of New Island South.

In the late 1990s and in 2001, surveys concluded there were three territorial pairs on the South reserve (W. Gibble & K. Gunther).
A survey carried out in early 2007 confirmed a minimum of six pairs breeding on the whole island.

Striated Caracara (Johnny Rook) *Phalcoboenus australis*
IUCN Red List Status: Near Threatened

The Johnny Rook is a rare species in World terms, and one of the main biodiversity values of New Island. The species was absent from New Island as a breeding bird when the island was taken over in 1972, and only a very small number of pairs nested in the surrounding smaller islands. This was the result of an intensive persecution before the creation of the reserve.

Census Work

A Falkland Islands-wide survey was made in 1983/1986 which gave a total figure of seven breeding pairs for New Island. In 1996 the total count and estimate was 14 pairs ("The Striated Caracara in the Falkland Islands", I.J. Strange, 1996).

A very detailed census initiated in the breeding season of 2005 and completed in January 2007 indicates that the present Striated caracara population comprises ca. 85 territorial pairs (not all of which nest in each year), plus more than one 100 non-territorial immature individuals on New Island (the whole island).

Breeding success of this population is very high (most successful pairs raising 2 or 3 chicks), which may be contributing to the rapid population growth recorded in the recent decades.

Ongoing studies indicate that the Striated Caracara on New Island feeds on a variety of prey, from beetles to rabbits, to Fur seal placentas and excrement. During the breeding season, prions and Upland geese (taken as carrion) seem to make up an important part of the diet.

Photo above: A Striated Caracara on the nest with chicks;
Photo left: the natural curiosity of these birds often leads to them being misunderstood and wrongly viewed as pests

Above: Distribution of Striated Caracara pairs with territories on the New Island South reserve in the breeding season of 2005/06. Survey carried out by Dr Paulo Catry.

Red-backed Buzzard *Buteo polyosoma*
This raptor is relatively scarce on New Island, with an estimate of three pairs nesting on the South reserve in most years since 1975.

Red-backed buzzards feed mostly on rabbits, also taking rats and mice. Pellets from this species confirm that they also take prions, but this is probably more opportunistic than deliberate preying.

Turkey Vulture *Cathartes aura*
This species nests in some numbers on New Island and surrounding islets, despite the fact that no sheep or cattle are present. In the absence of other carrion, Turkey vultures are regularly seen scavenging corpses of rabbits, Upland geese, penguins and other birds, and they are often seen amongst Fur seal colonies. No information is available on the numbers present, other than that groups of more than 6 birds are rarely seen (but up to 19 individuals were observed in one area, on one occasion, in January 2006).

Waders, Skuas, Gulls and Terns

Pied or Magellanic Oystercatcher
Haematopus leucopodus (photo below)
This sedentary wader is common on New Island and along most coasts in the Falkland Islands.

Census Work
During October-December 2004 a relatively detailed survey was carried out which resulted in the location of 30 pairs with eggs and/or broods (not counting second broods) on New Island South. A further two to four territorial pairs were noticed, bringing the population to 32-34 pairs and 10-15 non-territorial flocking individuals. Numbers in other years were similar, but counts were less precise and exhaustive.

Breeding success on New Island South is variable, almost nil in some years (e.g. in 2003), but fairly good in others (e.g. in 2005). Many nests and broods seem to suffer from predation, which is not surprising considering the large numbers of skuas and Striated caracaras present on the island.

Blackish Oystercatcher *Haematopus ater*
The Blackish oystercatcher is sedentary and widespread in the Falkland Islands.

On New Island South the species is present on both the eastern sheltered coast and on the exposed western shores. Unlike the Magellanic oystercatcher, it not only nests on level ground but also on shelves, high above the sea, on the precipitous western cliffs. Given these habitat choices, they are relatively hard to count accurately.

Combining observations made in 2004 and 2005, with several nests or broods found, the local breeding population is

Photo left: Two-banded Plover (immature)

estimated at 16 pairs (with a few more non-breeding individuals).

Two-banded Plover *Charadrius falklandicus*

These small and sedentary waders are notoriously difficult to count and no detailed surveys have been made of their population on New Island South. The main nesting areas are around Ferguson's Paddock and Beef Island Point, but nests can also be found around Whalebone Beach, the airstrip, at Eddy Point and on higher ground above the Settlement. For some years before 1983, several pairs nested on bare open ground within the Settlement, but since re-vegetation, birds have vacated this area.

On 8 November 1996 a coastal survey covering New Island South, gave a total of 36 individuals.
A maximum total of 81 individuals was recorded during the coastal survey in early February 2004, at the end of the breeding season, but this included several fledglings. The number of nesting pairs is estimated at somewhere between 25 and 40.

Falkland Skua *Catharacta skua antarctica*

Falkland skuas are migratory seabirds that live a pelagic life during winter. In the summer breeding season, birds return to New Island around mid to late October and remain until late March. On New Island, skuas are numerous and the island is probably one of the most important breeding grounds for this species in the archipelago. Here, one of the main food sources for the skua is the Thin-billed Prion; several thousands may be taken every breeding season.

Census Work

A detailed survey was first made of the species between 3-23 December 1996 when pairs holding territories with nests were counted. A total of 280 pairs were found and mapped on New Island South, but not defined with GPS.

A further detailed census of this species was carried out between 12-20 December 2004 (during the last part of egg-laying). A total of 417 territorial pairs (most of them with nests) were located on New Island South. The central position of each territory (or nest, when found) was determined using GPS and a detailed distribution map produced.

Research

Since 2003, data has been systematically collected on the breeding biology, diet and several aspects of the behaviour of this species. Special loggers called geolocators (small devices used to study migration) were deployed on several birds, which allowed, for the first time, the identification of the migration routes and wintering areas of Falkland skuas. It was surprising to find that skuas live highly pelagic winter lives, far from the coast, mostly above deep shelf-break and oceanic waters north of the Falklands (Phillips et al. submitted). Further research is being carried out including morphometrics and the winter ecology (based on stable isotope analyses) of the two sexes.

Dolphin Gull *Larus scoresbii*
The Dolphin gull is fairly widespread in the coastal areas of the Falkland Islands. On New Island South this species breeds in variable numbers, often shifting nesting sites from one year to the next.
Dolphin gulls appear to be mainly tidal foragers on New Island, but are always present amongst nesting cormorants, Rockhopper penguins and Gentoo penguins scavenging on excreta and regurgitated food.

In 2003, 60 pairs nested on a cliff ledge west of the Settlement Rookery and 12 pairs nested at Eddy Point.
In 2004, the only nesting site was at Eddy Point (mixed colony with Kelp Gulls), where up to 200 adults were seen and between 60 and 120 nests were estimated to have been built.
In 2005, 72 pairs nested at Eddy Point and an estimated 65 pairs nested by Cave Cliff, on ledges in a deep gulch on the west side of Landsend Bluff, bringing the local nesting population to 137 pairs in that year.

Photo below: Dolphin Gulls near Grand Cliff

Dominican or Kelp Gull
Larus dominicanus
Kelp gulls are year-round residents on the Falkland Islands. Numbers nesting on New Island South vary annually, as a result of birds regularly moving colony sites.

In the past three years (2003, 2004 and 2005) the main nesting site has been at Eddy Point, at the South end of New Island. The maximum counts for this colony in each year are as follows:

- 2003: 175 adults   49 nests
- 2004: 457 adults   -
- 2005: 800 adults   99 nests

Two other colonies were located in 2005: two nests with eggs at Beef Island Point; and an estimated 35 pairs nesting on the west side of the island's cliffs near Landsend Bluff, bringing the New Island South breeding population to 136 pairs in this year.

South American Tern
Sterna hirundinacea
This migratory species is widespread and relatively numerous along the coast of the Falkland Islands and South America. On New Island South, terns are relatively scarce, but their numbers can fluctuate widely between years and times of the season.
In 2001, a small colony of these terns formed on a beach immediately east of Strong Tide Point, numbering 25 nests.
In 2003, 2004 and 2005 there were no attempts at nesting made on New Island South and terns were in general very scarce, although occasionally flocks of a few dozen could be found foraging close inshore or roosting on rocks by the shore.

Owls

Short-eared Owl *Asio flammeus*
These owls are widespread but relatively scarce on the Falkland Islands, being found mostly on small offshore islands. Short-eared owls on New Island are generally flushed from dense areas of Cinnamon Grass or Blue Grass, where they have been known to nest.

Breeding on New Island has been occasionally confirmed (most recently in 2003) but the population is undoubtedly small, maybe three to four pairs on the South reserve.

Photo above: Dark-faced Ground Tyrant

Passerines

Dark-faced Ground Tyrant
Muscisaxicola macloviana
On New Island, tyrants are widespread and common, but perhaps more numerous near cliffs and on higher ground.
Tyrants nest in rocky outcrops and have been found nesting in the crevices of stone walls in the Settlement. Although no survey data is available for the early 1970s, this may be one species which perhaps has seen a small decline on New Island when sheep were removed. A common food source for tyrants was the "Bluebottle" fly, which has greatly reduced in numbers due to the absence of sheep.

Grass Wren *Cistothorus platensis*
The Grass wren is one of several species that, in the Falkland Islands, seems to be somewhat affected by the presence of introduced predators. On New Island South it is one of the scarcest breeding birds, which is also a consequence of the shortage of habitats with long grass-like vegetation, such as Tussac stands.

Between 5 and 7 pairs may nest in the Settlement Rookery Tussac (occasionally also observed in *Poa alopecurus* stands). This species is also present in the South End Tussac.

Photo above: Short-eared Owl in Tussac

Photo above: A Falkland Thrush, nesting in one of the settlement sheds

Falkland Thrush *Turdus falcklandii*
This common and widespread species is more abundant around the Settlement (where it nests in sheds and other buildings), in Gorse *Ulex europaea* and in areas covered by Tussac grass. Thrushes can also be found nesting on the ground. It is also frequently found on higher ground and near cliffs, but is scarce or absent from lowland rolling or flat areas without taller vegetation or rocky outcrops.

Falkland Pipit *Anthus correndera*
Despite their widespread distribution in the Falkland Islands, pipits were absent from New Island in the early 1970s, probably due to overgrazing of the area. Since the creation of the nature reserve and the removal of sheep, the vegetation has shown a remarkable recovery and pipits have come back. They are now relatively widespread and not uncommon in most of the lowland areas of New Island South, being clearly associated with areas of grasses, such as *Holcus*.

Tussac Bird *Cinclodes antarcticus*
Tussac birds on New Island are fairly widespread, but not numerous. An exceptionally tame and inquisitive species, which spends a lot of time on the ground seeking food, Tussac birds are particularly vulnerable to introduced predators on New Island.

Census Work
Systematic atlas work all over New Island South in October/November 2004 resulted in Tussac birds being recorded in 21 of 59 (500 x 500m) quadrants surveyed. The survey revealed that birds had a clear bias towards coastal areas with tall cliffs and gulches. A rough estimate, based on these surveys, points to a population of 20-30 breeding pairs.

Long-tailed Meadowlark
Sturnella loyca
This is a relatively common and widespread bird on New Island South, particularly numerous around the Settlement.

In 2004 five nesting sites were found in the Settlement, within an area of 300m^2. In 2006 a similar density was found, with pairs bringing out two broods. Often found nesting in the cover of Cinnamon Grass, now a common plant since the removal of stock. Meadowlarks can be found from the coast to the high ground, but they are scarce or absent in some areas of the reserve.

Photo below: A male Long-tailed Meadowlark in Gorse

Black-throated Finch
Melanodera melanodera
This finch is widespread and relatively common on most of the Falkland Islands. On New Island South, however, it is scarce and localised, having only been recorded for the first time in recent years and possibly increasing.

In 2003 and 2004 Black-throated finches nested on Beef Island Point, on Coffin Island Point and possibly also on Eddy Point.
In 2005 this species also nested in Tussac areas on Rookery Hill.
The total New Island South population is estimated at less than 10 pairs.

Black-chinned Siskin *Carduelis barbata*
This small finch is usually only found in the Settlement area of New Island, although some individuals are sporadically seen moving through or feeding in other parts of the island.

Siskins nest in gorse, *Hebe* and *Cuppressus macrocarpa* trees. The number of breeding pairs in the Settlement in 2003 was estimated at less than five.
In February 2004, when many fledglings were present, the total population was estimated at 20 to 40 birds.

Vagrants

A considerable number of vagrant and annual visiting birds are recorded on New Island. Between 1972 and 2006, 36 different species of vagrant have been recorded on the island by Ian Strange. This does not include seabirds passing the island or species that may have been observed on New Island North.

The most commonly recorded species are:

- **Chilean Swallow** *Tachycieta leucopyga*
- **North American Barn Swallow** *Hirundo rustica erythrogaster*
- **Violet Eared Dove** *Zenaida auriculata*
- **Cattle Egret** *Bubulcus ibis*
- **Rufous-collared (Chingolo) Sparrow** *Zonotrichia capensis*
- **Buff-necked Ibis** *Theristicus caudatus melanopis*
- **Rufous-backed Negrito** *Lessonia rufa*

Sea Lion

Mammals

There are no native land mammals in the Falkland Archipelago, but several have been introduced. Marine mammals however are fairly diverse and abundant, and the New Island reserve protects an important percentage of the Islands' breeding population of the Falkland Islands Fur seal, and is an important feeding ground for a number of other marine mammals.

Cetaceans

Of the larger whales that are to be found in Falkland waters, Southern Right Whales *Eubalaena australis* and Sei Whales *Balaenoptera borealis* are the ones seen most often from New Island. Occasionally they have been observed in shallow waters, within a few metres of the shore. Sei and Fin Whales *Balaenoptera physalus* are most often seen in mid to late summer, sometimes in large numbers, as they migrate north. The numbers of these whales observed off New Island have increased in the last decade from their general decline in Falkland waters around the mid 1960s when spasmodic whaling was being carried out by Russian whaling fleets. Smaller cetaceans such as the Southern Right Whale Dolphin *Lissodelphis peronii*, and the Hourglass Dolphin *Lagenorhynchus cruciger*, have also been recorded at New Island.

Killer Whale or Orca
Orcinus orca
Observed in small numbers close inshore, but only on a few occasions each summer. However, their apparent preference for the west side of the island probably influences the numbers being recorded. A group of seven animals, the largest recorded to date at New Island, was observed close inshore at the Settlement Rookery landing area in December 2006.

Pilot Whale
Globicephala melaena
The only record of this whale in New Island waters is a stranding of some 50 animals which occurred in Settlement Harbour on Protector Beach on 10 March 1990 (Shona Strange, pers. comm.). This is one of the few strandings of this species carefully documented where animals were successfully re-floated and swam away.

Peale's Dolphin or Peale's Porpoise

Lagenorhychus australis
Photo above: Peale's porpoises close inshore

The seas around New Island are quite rich in cetaceans, of which the most common is the Peale's Porpoise, regularly seen playing, feeding or resting very close inshore. In mid-summer, they can be seen on a daily basis, often including very small calves.

Commerson's Dolphin
Cephalorhynchus commersonii
This species is uncommon in New Island harbours, although common amongst the nearby harbours of Weddell and Beaver Islands. Very occasionally they can be seen at New Island, often in company with the Peale's Porpoise.

Sea Lions and Seals

Two species of seal occur regularly on New Island: the Falkland Islands Fur seal *Arctocephalus australis* and the Southern Sea Lion *Otaria flavescens*.
Two other species: the Southern Elephant Seal *Mirounga leonina* and the Leopard Seal *Hydrurga leptonyx* *(photo below)* are occasional visitors.

Sea Lion *Otaria flavescens*
Sea Lions are seen in small numbers (including adult males, adult females, and immatures) around many areas of New Island's coastline on a regular basis. Between 10 and 20 animals may haul out around the shoreline in summer, with larger numbers in winter, and they are often observed fishing near the shore along the edge of *Macrocystis* kelp beds, where they take octopus and bottom dwelling fish. Sea Lions are also seen preying on Gentoo and Rockhopper penguins as these birds come ashore.

Sea lions have suffered a catastrophic decline in the Falklands during most of the 20th century ("Sea Lion Survey in the Falklands", I.J. Strange, 1979; Thompson et al. 2005).

Previous owners of New Island are known to have persecuted and shot this species. From the description of Fergus O'Gorman, who visited New Island in late April and early May 1960, one deduces that many hundreds of Sea Lion were then present (he counted 260 individuals and wrote about "several hundred" more in a different place).

Today, Sea Lions do not breed regularly on New Island, but possibly breed in small numbers on the nearby islands of Ship, Beef, Saddle and Coffin.

Falkland Islands Fur seal
Arctocephalus australis australis
New Island holds one of the most important Fur seal rookeries in the Falklands, one of 10 known breeding places in the archipelago. There are three separate rookeries on New Island. Total numbers are very difficult to estimate, not only due to the fact that at any one time many of the seals will be foraging at sea, but also because pups keep hidden most of the time, under boulders or rock overhangs.

Census Work
A count carried out on 23 December 2005, towards the end of the pupping season, yielded 1,280 individuals (adults and sub-adults, excluding pups; of these 855 were on the north side of Landsend Bluff, and 425 on the south side of Landsend Bluff).

Photo left: A bull Sea Lion with a Gentoo Penguin

At the same time, 257 pups were recorded, but this figure has relatively little meaning, since pups were still being born, and many others were invisible as they hid amongst boulders. Many pups were on their own, as females were at sea.

A relatively new breeding site located just to the north of Settlement Rookery on the West Cliffs was, in late December 2006, estimated to hold approximately 200 adult and sub-adult animals.
The total number of Fur seals on the New Island rookeries is estimated at around 2,000 animals.

A survey was carried out in late April and early May 1960 by O'Gorman who "generously estimated" the New Island population at 4,500 individuals (O'Gorman, 1960). However, counts made at this time of the year on New Island can be high due to influxes of immature animals.

Given the difficulty of counting seals on New Island and the different times of the year at which counts were made, it is difficult to compare this figure with more recent counts. All that can be said is that Fur seal numbers have not suffered marked changes in the past 45 years, and based on their spreading to new areas of coast, are probably increasing. Such increases are in line with increases observed at other sites in the Falkland Islands (I.J. Strange, 1990).

Photo below: A breeding group of Falkland Islands Fur seal on New Island, including the Harem male and a newly born pup

Cottontail rabbit on Gorse

Non-native Species

As a result of New Island's long history of occupation by man since around 1774, it is not surprising that it is not free of introduced mammals or plants. Today, with a great deal more attention being given world-wide to non-native species, the presence of certain non-native mammals on the island is the subject of some debate. However, on the positive side, New Island is offering a unique opportunity to study the effects of its introduced species and to make known its interesting findings on this subject.

Mammals

Cottontail Rabbit
Eastern Cottontail *Sylvilagus floridanus*
Cottontail rabbits are widespread in North America and were brought to New Island by early North American sealers or whalers (from original log books, Nantucket Historical Association).

Today they are still fairly widespread, being particularly numerous in and around the Settlement as well as over most medium and high altitude areas on South Hill, but scarce to the north of the island.

Grazers as they are, they probably still have some localised impact on the vegetation, but their numbers are a fraction today of what they were when sheep were also grazing the island and the vegetation was much shorter.

The precise identification of the species of Cottontail rabbit present on New Island has not yet been made. At least two introductions at different periods are recorded.
In a reference to finding Captain Barnard and his men, it is evident that one of these introductions was prior to 1814.
In an extract from the log of James Choyce of the *Asp* dated the 23 November 1814 he recorded how Barnard had survived and wrote "There were great quantities of rabbits, ducks and geese" which were taken for food.

A further introduction was made in the 1820s by Captain William Horton Smyley. ("The Falkland Islands", I.J. Strange, 1972).

Feral Cat *Felis domesticus*
Cats are likely to have been present on New Island at least since the times when the Whaling Station was active; that is, for some 98 years, or more. A photograph taken while the 1908-1916 whaling station was in operation, shows a whaler holding a cat, which is the first positive evidence of their presence.

A photograph taken in 1925 has a reference to "the thirty cats, brought in to keep the rats down from the Whaling Station" ("Penguins and Seashore Friends", Dolly Penguin, 1992).

Other residents of New Island from the 1920s to 1950s confirm that domesticated cats were kept and fed, but they have no recollection of feral cats (pers. comm. Teen Short, F. Ferguson, Olga Coutts).

In the 1960s there is a reference to some 30 cats being brought in specifically to reduce the number of prions (pers. comm. J. Davis). That prions were the subject of intense persecution on New Island in the 1960s is borne out by the 1964 Wild Animals and Birds Protection Ordinance. Prions were removed from the list of protected species and were placed on the list of birds that could be killed at any time, specifically for the benefit of the New Island owners of that time.

When the New Island Preservation Company took over in 1972, feral cats were still evident. Currently there are no cats living in association with humans on New Island, and the feral cats present never get any food from direct human sources.

They are relatively wild, shy creatures, found from the Settlement area to remote bluffs and the top of the higher hills. Most kittens seem to be born in November and December (based on the observation of seven families in 2005). They vary in colour from light ginger tabby to black or tortoiseshell.

Photo below: A feral cat on New Island

The overall density of cats on New Island is low; in a report "Eradication of Problem Animals in the Falkland Islands", a New Zealand eradication expert, Brian Bell, who visited New Island on 9-12 July 1995 wrote that "cats are present but appear to be in relatively small numbers". Systematic observations in the Settlement area (where reproducing females are easily found) suggest a density of 8-10 cats per km^2 in this particular area. This is especially high due to the dense cover provided by Gorse, and a higher density of Cottontail rabbits, rats and mice which is their main feed.

Sightings have been especially low in other areas. In 2003 when field workers walked some 500km checking survey rat traps throughout New Island South, only seven cats were identified.

In the summer of 2006, following a particularly wet winter, (50mm above normal rainfall being recorded), only five cats were identified. On this basis alone, the population on New Island is probably less than 50 cats.

Research

A study of cat diet was carried out in the summer seasons of 2004 and 2005. Results of this study (Matias & Catry) and a stable-isotope investigation (Quillfeldt et al. submitted) consistently indicate that cats on New Island feed primarily on rabbits, rats, mice and prions, with other birds and invertebrates playing a minor role in the diet. Relatively crude calculations suggest that cats kill only a small proportion of the prion population each season. Prions are only available to cats when ashore for breeding between October and early March.

Presently under investigation is also the relationship of the exotic disease Tularemia, found in Cottontails, which is also known to affect cats. This could be a factor influencing the feral cat population on New Island.

Black Rat *Rattus rattus*

New Island is so far the only island in the Falklands where the Ship rat or Black rat has been discovered. How or when it was originally introduced is not clear, although circumstantial evidence suggests it could have been between the years 1906-1916 when the whaling industry was operational.

An extract from the writings of Mrs D. McRae, a resident on New Island at the time the whaling station closed in 1916, records one effect of the closure:

"Rats of all shapes, sizes and colour" without

food from the station "started to roam the island, so our cats had to soon earn their keep" - a strong inference that rats were not present before the establishment of the whaling station.

Today the species is mostly associated with Tussac stands, the Settlement buildings and Gorse, probably linked to the fact that it prefers cover where it can climb (Prof. William Henry Burt, University of Michigan). Although also occurring in other areas, such as cliff tops with only short vegetation, rats are relatively scarce there.

Research

An extensive programme of trapping was carried out in 2001-2004, when a total of 11,015 trap days (total number of days on which traps were set) was recorded. In the 2002 season (4,270 trap days, the highest of the four periods) a total of 157 rats and 204 mice were caught.

Open areas, which are the most extensively occurring habitat on the island, had very low densities of rats and mice. In contrast, areas providing cover in the form Tussac grass *Parodiochloa flabellata* or Gorse contained considerable numbers of both species of rodents (Schenk et al. submitted)

From extensive analysis of stomach contents, rats on New Island are known to feed mainly (70-80%) on vegetation during the early part of the summer season (Schenk et al. submitted). Three percent of the total samples taken contained traces of ingested birds: three feathers; and two egg yolks (from Rockhopper penguin eggs). However, preliminary data indicate the proportion of ingested birds, including scavenged, was much higher in the Prion chick-rearing period (Quillfeldt et al. submitted), in all areas except the Rookery Tussac area. The current impact of rats on the overall prion population however, seems to be low (P. Catry et al. 2006), (Quillfeldt et al. submitted).

It is possible that rats, together with other introduced predators, might be responsible for the absence from New Island of small petrel species such as Diving petrels and Storm petrels; and of other small breeding birds such as the Cobb's wren. On the other

Photo above: Volunteer and PhD student, Riek van Noordwijk, making housings for rat traps

hand there is no evidence that these species did in fact inhabit New Island before the introduction of rats.

The increase of other ground nesting species, such as pipits, meadowlarks, thrushes and the return of Black-throated finches since the removal of sheep, is also an important factor to take into account when rodent predation is considered.

House Mouse *Mus musculus*

Research

Mice were included in a stable-isotope investigation of introduced mammals at New Island (Quillfeldt et al. submitted). While most of the 14 mice in the study had a mainly terrestrial diet according to their isotope ratios, several mice had isotope ratios in a position intermediate between terrestrial and marine values, indicative of a mixed diet, and one mouse from an open upland area grouped with the marine data for muscle isotope ratios, indicating a specialisation of this latter mouse in marine-derived food (Quillfeldt et al. submitted).

Mice were caught in all trap lines, including open heathland, but were more abundant in areas with cover provided by Gorse and particularly Tussac, (see: Black Rat - Research, Pg. 77).

The impact of mice on the fauna and flora of New Island is presently not known, nor is anything known about their introduction to the island, but further work on this non-native species is planned for the future.

Plants

Gorse
Ulex europaeus

Gorse also has to be considered as an introduced non-native species and one that is probably very important when the impact of other introduced species is considered. Gorse was introduced to East Falkland as early as 1847. On West Falkland, records indicate that the first introduction took place around 1881.

On New Island, Gorse has existed for nearly 100 years, with the main growth around the Settlement and at the site of the old whaling station. A few small individual bushes are located at some five coastal sites elsewhere on the island.

Since the removal of sheep, existing bushes have increased their ground cover, which, in the last 25 years, is estimated to have increased by approximately 50%. Sheep, and possibly cattle, were known to graze the new shoots of Gorse.

Cottontail rabbits graze this shrub and breed under its dense cover. Mice, Black rats, cats, nesting Thrushes and Siskins all co-habit

Photo left: A Cottontail rabbit feeding on Gorse

Photo above: Gorse clearing - a programme of partial eradication was carried out on New Island South during the 2006 season, to reduce Gorse cover by fifty percent in the Settlement area

gorse. The frequent presence of Turkey Vultures around the Settlement Gorse areas may indicate that they also nest under the cover of this shrub.

Elsewhere in the Falklands, Gorse is used as a nesting habitat for increasing numbers of breeding Barn Owls (R.B. Napier and W. Pole-Evans pers. comm.).

Because Gorse is an introduced species there are views expressed, especially by New Zealand non-native species specialists, that it should be removed from the Falkland Islands generally. New Zealand is known to have problems with rampant Gorse, but this is not the case in the climate of the Falkland Islands. A visit to New Island by a New Zealand introduced species specialist in November 2006, confirmed that the growth and form of this plant here bears no resemblance to its growth in New Zealand. In the Falkland Islands its aesthetic values are appreciated in all settlements, especially in spring when its bright yellow flowers add colour to the scene. However, as one of the prime habitats for non-native species, and as a high fire risk, a programme of partial eradication of Gorse on New Island was carried out in the 2006 season. The aim of this was to reduce Gorse cover on the island by 50%, thereby limiting its further increase.

Total eradication of Gorse on the island is neither a practical nor desirable option. Many areas of Gorse could not be easily cleared, and, as previously mentioned, it also provides a valuable nesting habitat for many native species.

Introduction of Livestock

It is a curious fact, that when the impact of non-native species is mentioned in the context of damage to the environment and to native species, there is little or no mention of those introduced animals such as sheep, cattle, pigs, horses, goats or dogs.

The first record of a dog on New Island goes back to the time of Captain Barnard in 1812. In one reference, dated 1872, there is mention of nine goats remaining on the island, from the Smith Brothers settlement of 1860.

The impact, especially by sheep and pigs, was found to be unbelievably high when the island was taken over by NIPCO in 1972/73. Irreparable damage was done, not just to the land and vegetation, but directly and indirectly to the island's native species. Today, concern is expressed at the possible impact of tourists on the nest burrows of prions, but for 140 years or more, the cloven feet of a large number of sheep trampled and broke into the same nest burrows, causing untold damage.

The first record of pigs being introduced was in 1812, by Captain Charles Barnard when two pigs, a sow and a boar, were brought from Swan Island (Weddell Island) and released at the South end of New Island. It is also recorded that in 1850 pigs were brought from the Cape Verde Islands by Captain Clift, of the whaler *Hudson*.
In a letter to the Secretary of State, William Marcy, dated 20 March 1854 relating to the introduction of different species by American whale ships and in defence of an American whaling captain in court for killing the same, Captain W. Smyley states:
"The British Government has never put an animal on any island but one since they had

Photo below: The North end of New Island in the mid 1970s, showing large areas of erosion caused by overgrazing

them, except for two worn out horses as pensioners for their good services, left on New Island". These were most likely the two "pack horses" used by Captain Campbell of the *Levenside* in 1851 for collecting guano. (See: Guano Industry, Pg. 15).

Since the removal of these species, in particular sheep, and as a result of better land management, New Island has been transformed from a virtual desert to a richly vegetated environment. Plants not recorded before have appeared and new species of breeding bird, especially ground nesters, are increasing.

The Impact of Livestock Removal on Non-native Mammals

Applying experience as a precedence and "ground level values" over scientific data, which is not available for earlier periods, the removal of sheep also affected some other non-native species. Cottontail rabbits, which were not only widespread but in large numbers, declined as the vegetation increased.

Originally, in the 1970s, feral cats were shot, but when it appeared they preyed mainly on rabbits and were also declining naturally, this practice stopped.

The removal of sheep was probably a major factor in reducing the rat population on New Island, as sheep provided a food source for these rodents. Additionally, baiting, which continues annually as a management policy, almost certainly was, and perhaps remains, an important factor in lowering the rat population.

In the case of mice, the situation is less clear. Mice make up a much higher percentage of the rodents trapped and are common in open areas where rats are not. Whether their populations have also been reduced is not known, but it is very doubtful.

A Natural Predatory Balance

A theory also based largely on ground level values and one which is indeed now being supported by scientific data, is that there could be a natural predatory balance which has developed between cats, rats, mice and rabbits. The decision to stop shooting cats was largely due to this theory, (supported by observations), that the main prey of cats are in fact rodents and rabbits.

Photos above, from left: Vanilla Daisy; Lady's Slipper; Marsh Daisy. Many species of flora such as these have returned to the island since the removal of livestock

Possible Impact of Introduced Mammals and Plants

Photo above: A Cottontail rabbit in Yorkshire Fog

It is fair to state that this is a subject of very considerable debate, not only worldwide, but even on New Island itself. Those who come to study here, who may have seen the effects of introduced mammals on different islands elsewhere in the world, will probably have different views to those with experience of this island. Even within the Falkland Islands, experiences and knowledge gained in different areas varies greatly and results in quite widely ranging views on this matter.

The very subject of non-native species is both emotive and political. In the past, man was responsible for many of these introductions. In the case of New Island, some were accidental, such as mice and rats. Rabbits, pigs, sheep and cattle were introduced as a means of survival for man. Cats were introduced initially as a form of pleasure for humans, and later as a form of control for introduced and native species.

Two or three decades ago, the subject of invasive species was not a priority and rarely raised. Today, it seems to be on the agenda of many political debates, and governments make allowances in their budgets for the control of invasive species. In general this is good, but is this relatively new policy of eradication of non-native species workable everywhere, and should more caution be applied before it is carried out?

In the case of New Island, the level of concern on the question of introduced species varies depending on individual experience. The situation on New Island today bears absolutely no relation to the despoliation that was found by those who came to the island to establish it as a wildlife reserve 35 years ago, and in relative terms, the possible impact of introduced species on the island now, is minor.

Even at this stage when a considerable amount of data has been collected by a number of different field workers on the remaining non-native species, there are many questions to be answered:

• Exactly what effect are the introduced species having on New Island's native species?

• What is the degree of impact?

• Are these populations regulated by each other?

• Are the present control methods sufficient?

What is clear, is that on New Island we have a unique situation with its remaining introduced species and it cannot be treated like any other island.

As an Important Bird Area (IBA) the New Island management will one day, no doubt, find themselves under intense political pressure to introduce an eradication programme.

The outstanding question remains as to whether we have sufficient knowledge to guarantee that any major eradication programme will be successful, not just for one species, but for all. Make one mistake in this respect and New Island's advances in the control of these non-native species might be reversed with serious consequences.

Photo below: A Striated caracara (immature) feeding on a rabbit

Photo above: PhD student Riek van Noordwijk working with King Cormorants at the main Settlement rookery

Research Strategy

Consistent with the New Island Conservation Trust memorandum, there is a long and fruitful tradition of research activities on the island which has resulted in many excellent science papers and reports. The facilities presently available on New Island are enough to accommodate several researchers each summer season. It is foreseeable that other research teams or individuals will express the wish and seek permission and support to work on the reserve in the future. The following section covers research aims and priorities for the New Island reserve.

Aims

There are a number of scientific programmes currently under way on New Island. These have been discussed and agreed with the island management and trustees, and their continuity to the end of the agreed working plans will not be questioned by the present research strategy.

However, given the increasing approaches by researchers interested in conducting work on New Island, it is advisable to define some strategic guidelines for the future. The aim of this exercise is not to narrow down the research possibilities or to exclude any type of research ideas, but rather to put an emphasis on research lines. These should be in the best interests of the management of the reserve, for the conservation of Falkland Islands biodiversity and for the monitoring of the marine environment surrounding the islands.

Defining Priorities

Research priorities will always be debatable and no two individuals are perhaps likely to share exactly the same point of view. However, sooner or later, reserve management will face decisions resulting from limited accommodation and other resources in relation to the huge potential for scientific work that New Island presents.

It is also important to remember that a scientific research priority may not be a priority of infrastructure management. For the reserve management and infrastructure to operate, it requires some support from research, otherwise research does not function.

Decisions on research projects will naturally depend not only on the projects themselves, but also on the individuals proposing to carry them out. Such decisions involve a degree of subjectivity that cannot be captured in a document such as this management plan. However, as guidance for decision-makers, the following broad guidelines are offered, identifying the kind of research programme that should be given priority:

• Research issues with clear and direct implications on the management or on fund-raising for the reserve. Examples would include issues such as the impact of alien species (including plants) on native taxa or the impact of human activities on the island.

• Research activities relevant to the monitoring of the marine environment surrounding New Island (including research focusing on the foraging and movements of marine birds).

The above, concerning the marine environment, is important in the wider context of the Falkland Islands and the Patagonian Shelf region, and might contribute to inform policy decision-makers at a broader level. The potential exploration and exploitation of the Special Co-Operation Area (SCA) is an example.

Researchers on New Island have already carried out some years of work, involving the satellite tracking of three species of penguin, (namely Rockhoppers, Magellanics and Gentoos) which demonstrates the importance of the SCA as a feeding ground for some of these species.

Such research may also contribute to the protection of the marine resources critical to the birds and mammals reproducing on the reserve (See: "Applying ecology to conservation: tracking breeding penguins at New Island South reserve, Falkland Islands", Boersma, Stokes & Strange, 2002).

There are a few species for which New Island represents a site of national and international importance. As such, the reserve has a special responsibility towards the wider community to the study, monitoring and conservation of the populations present within its limits. Identified species in this situation include:

Black-browed Albatross
Thalassarche melanophrys
This species is classified as Endangered (BirdLife International 2004), the most unfavourable global conservation status for any species occurring on the reserve. Interestingly, long-term counts on New Island have indicated a population increase. New Island might harbour near 1% of the world population, and as such should play an important role in its study, monitoring and conservation.

Thin-billed Prion
Pachyptila belcheri
New Island holds the largest recorded colony in the world for this species and a very large fraction of its national population. It is thanks to the huge numbers of prions it harbours that New Island can claim the status of the largest seabird colony in the Falklands, a valuable asset, and one which attracts much interest and gives access to potential funding sources for further research.

Current research on New Island is making a significant contribution towards the aim of using this species for the monitoring of the marine environment (Quillfeldt et al. 2003, Quillfeldt et al. 2006, Quillfeldt et al. 2007, Quillfeldt et al. in press).

Monitoring of the prion population is of utmost importance, given the ever present possibility that introduced mammals might, at some stage, become a threat to its conservation. As such, despite the fact that Thin-billed prions are not globally threatened, a high priority should be given to research focusing on biology and foraging ecology.

Gentoo Penguin
Pygoscelis papua
Before the mass mortality that occurred in 2002, New Island probably held more than 1% of the world population of this species that is currently classified as Near Threatened (BirdLife International 2004).
Although the relative importance of New Island is now diminished, it could still play a significant role in the conservation and monitoring of this species.

Magellanic Penguin
Spheniscus magellanicus
This species is decreasing in numbers in its global distribution and is currently classified as Near Threatened (BirdLife International 2004). The relative and absolute importance of the New Island population is unknown, but it is likely that the reserve harbours a significant proportion of the national population. The study and monitoring of this species will be significant, both for a better understanding of its population dynamics, and for interactions with the marine ecosystems surrounding New Island.

Rockhopper Penguin
Eudyptes chrysocome

Although the New Island population is small in world terms, it represents well over 1% of the national population of this globally threatened species, classified as Vulnerable by the IUCN Red List (BirdLife International 2004). There is a long tradition of research on this species on New Island and continued study and monitoring may contribute to an improved knowledge of population dynamics and of the marine environment on which these birds depend.

Striated Caracara/Johnny Rook
Phalcoboenus australis

New Island might harbour between 5 and 10% of the Falklands population and a significant fraction of the world population of this species classified as Near Threatened (BirdLife International 2004).
Its continued monitoring and study on New Island is a priority.

Terrestrial and Marine Ecology Studies

Plants and Invertebrates
There is little detailed knowledge on the plants and invertebrates of New Island. This is a field which is particularly important, considering the island's past history of spoliation and recent efforts to correct this.

Inshore Marine Environments
There is very little detailed information on the island's marine life and habitats. New Island would make an ideal location for such work.

Photo below: Gentoo penguins at the South End beach

Environmental Management Policies

New Island saw the start of environmental management 35 years ago in 1972, through basic and practical applications. Its main policy is a simple one: after some 200 years of spoliation by man, to give the island some respite and make it into a sanctuary for its wildlife.

New Island holds the largest seabird colony of the Falkland Islands. It harbours nationally and internationally important populations of several species, including Thin-billed prions, Black-browed albatross, Gentoo, Magellanic and Rockhopper penguins, Striated caracaras and Fur seal, and its coastal marine habitats are in a pristine state.

Terrestrial habitats on New Island have largely recovered from past depredations and the reserve represents the founding example of one of the largest areas in the Falklands where grazers have been completely removed.

The history of New Island, particularly in relation to the whaling era, is of national significance and many artefacts and historical records remain. The New Island reserve has a special responsibility in the conservation of this heritage and a significant role to play in both national and international contexts.

Ongoing management policies need to be specific for New Island. They should be based on the trial and error experiences of time and recognise national and international obligations, but without jeopardising past achievements.

New Island can be described as a natural "laboratory", where interactions between the effects of past and present human activities can be studied in a very favourable context. The number of monitoring and research projects on New Island is increasing and the reserve plays the leading role in environmental research in the Falkland Islands.

Photo opposite: Dusk over Cliff Knob Island from the New Island settlement

New Island is also an important tourist destination for ship-based visitors, particularly those on vessels and expeditions with a main focus on the natural environment.

The management objectives for the reserve and the detailed management prescriptions that follow, provide the framework for the NICT's decision making.

Management Objectives

• To conserve the native flora and fauna present on the reserve, particularly maintaining or increasing, as far as practical, population levels of the most relevant species in a national and international context.

• To monitor the impact of invasive species and to prepare plans, as far as practical, to stabilise or limit their populations, or, where suitable, to eradicate them.

• To prevent the introduction of further alien species, including plants, invertebrates and vertebrates as far as is practical.

• To manage and conserve, where practical, historical and archaeological features.

• To receive visitors and tourists, thus allowing the broader appreciation of the natural heritage of the sub-antarctic islands and sea, and the public dissemination of knowledge on conservation initiatives.

• To provide a base for, and to encourage high quality research by both scientific and naturalist personnel, particularly on themes applied to the management of the reserve and to relevant environmental monitoring in the Falkland Islands and surrounding seas.

• To use data gathered from New Island to lobby for the conservation of the marine areas and resources surrounding the island, which are vital to the conservation of marine mammals and seabirds reproducing on the reserve. To seek co-operation on these matters with other organisations and movements interested in marine conservation in West Falkland.

• To manage the reserve to ensure that the Falkland Islands Government's international obligations are met, where such obligations are feasible and appropriate to the long established aims of the reserve.

• To seek means of ensuring financial sustainability for the New Island operation, allowing a continuing presence on the island, which is necessary for management activities, as well as the continuation of long-term environmental monitoring schemes.

• To encourage and develop high ethical standards through non-invasive techniques in research and to foster generalised studies.

Photo below: Orea Anderson, carefully applying a ring to a young albatross

Researchers: Their Position and Responsibilities

Researchers play an important part in the concept and aims of the New Island reserve, but in the same way we look at the impact of visitors and tourists on the island's wildlife and its environment, no management plan should exclude the impact of field researchers.

The foundation stone for the work of present day researchers on New Island was started in 1973. It developed, not through the complex and intricate research we see today, but by field naturalists who looked at nature in the broader context. To prove things scientifically was not so important or such an issue as it today. As biological research advances, its methodology will change. Field research now dwells less on general observations with more attention given to complex issues in biology.

The techniques needed to carry out such studies have become more invasive on their study subjects and science should be under the same obligation as a tourist or visitor, and required to abide by common sense rules. We should all be reminded that through the eyes of a bird or an animal, there is no distinction between one human being and another!

Eventually, the author, himself a naturalist, would hope there could be a return to more basic field research, akin to what has been carried out over the past years. It should be a responsibility of not only the management, but also of the more academically directed field researchers to help promote this more basic, but never the less important work. Perhaps there is need to robustly impress on those in the academic world who set research parameters for PhD's, that the broader and more basic research is just as important and should not be denied to those seeking a degree in the natural sciences.

The New Island management has a policy of refusing permission to carry out certain research methods, but the line between what management might consider unacceptable and that a research worker might view as acceptable, can be a fine one, and thus extra consideration is needed from the researchers themselves.

It remains a policy of the New Island Reserve to encourage researchers who spend time on the island to assist in the general day to day upkeep of the facility.

Photo above: FIG Environmental Officer, Helen Otley, with Dr Petra Quillfeldt, working in the field with Thin-billed Prions

Distribution of Results

All researchers working on New Island and receiving support in one form or another from the Trust, commit themselves to the production of reports with relevant data to be submitted to the Trust and kept in its library and files.

The NICT has an obligation to present data to the Falkland Islands Government. Failing to present any significant outputs could jeopardise work in subsequent years and loss of status. The exact form of such reports will be dependent on the nature of the work being carried out and it seems unnecessary to adopt a specific form or database to be completed by scientists.
Please see Annex 8 for a full list of publications and papers produced in connection with research carried out on the New Island reserve.

Issuing of Permits and Support of Research Activities

Authorisation to carry out research activities on New Island lies with the management in consultation with the board of Trustees. Additional permission for any research to be carried out in the Falkland Islands must be obtained from the Falkland Islands Government Environmental Planning Department as required by law.

It has been Trust policy to give support in kind, in the form of accommodation, local transport, food supplies and fuel for heating and cooking to all research personnel working on New Island. However, the continuation of such practices may need to be revised, in order to guarantee the financial sustainability of the operation into the future.

Scientific Advisory Board

The ability shown by the NICT to produce high quality research and management of the reserve over a considerable number of years, raises the question of whether a scientific advisory board should be formed. To assist the Trustees in their decisions concerning the sound management of the reserve for conservation purposes, and the approval and regulation of research projects and activities, there is certainly a need to include people working on the reserve, both management and field scientists. However, the inclusion of others with less experience of the island, whilst providing an independent view, may also lead to unnecessary burdens.

Rockhopper penguins coming ashore at sunset

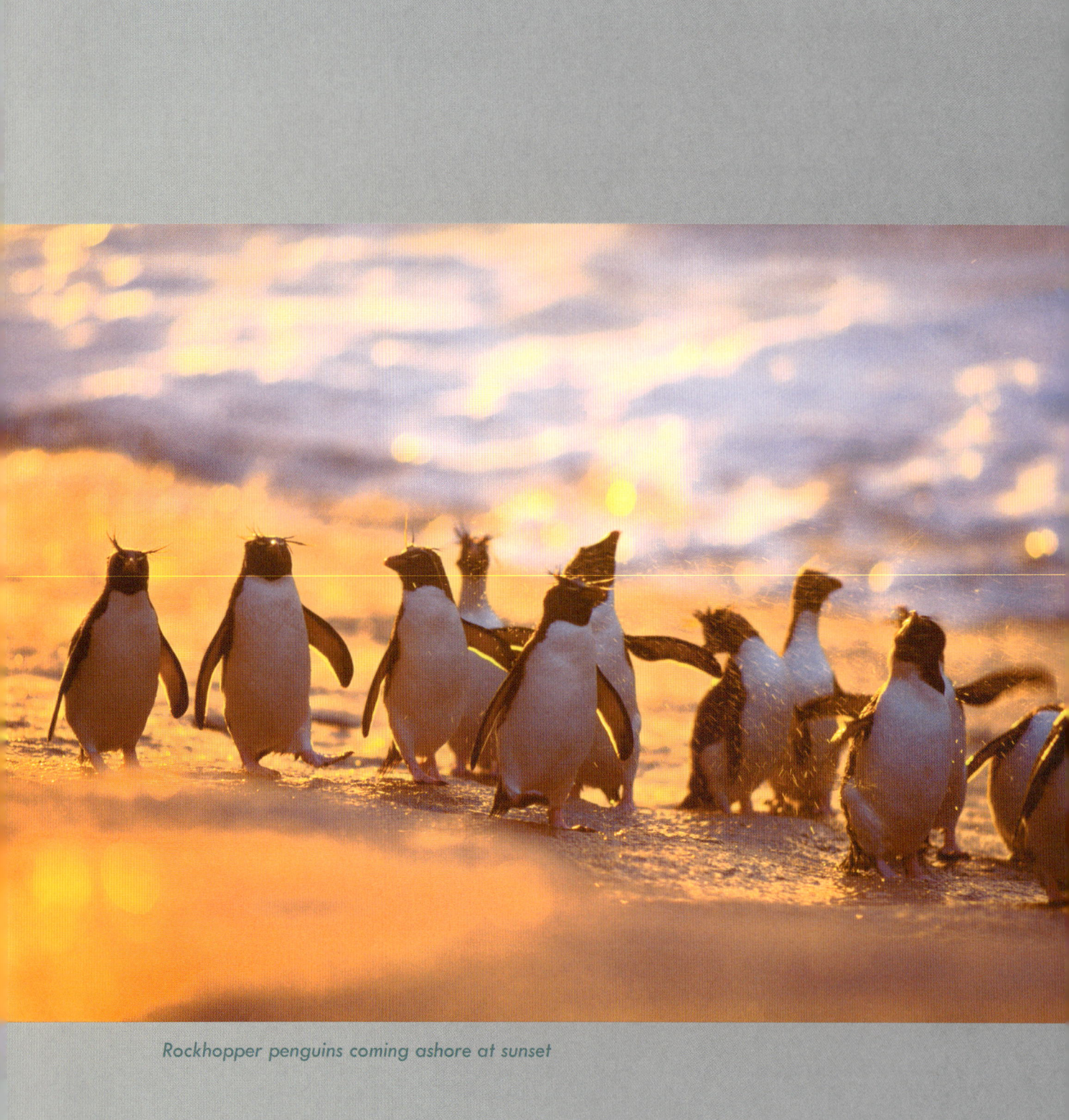

Conservation Policies

Part of the New Island Conservation Trust Memorandum reads:
To advance the education of the public in the ecology, conservation, history and other matters relating to the island.
Allowing tourists to visit New Island assists in this goal, but freedom to enjoy nature remains an important policy.

Tourism and Visitor Management

When the original concept for establishing New Island as a wildlife reserve was first conceived in 1972 it was a pioneering venture for the Falkland Islands. The preservation of its wildlife is foremost in this venture, but it is also important to offer it as a form of refuge for man, where nature can be enjoyed in its raw, relatively untouched state with a minimum of constraints.

Based on the understanding that after 200 years or more of spoliation by man, New Island could never regain its original pristine state, allowing visitors the same freedom as we were attempting to give wildlife was, and still is, a compatible venture.

With its years of ground experience in tourism and visitor operations, New Island has developed a baseline for such operations that is well suited to its own specific environment. It remains free of board-walks, notice boards and man-made barriers, thus allowing that extra freedom for visitors to enjoy nature. Guided only by common sense rules, such things remain key to this objective. Only by giving more people the opportunity to experience and appreciate the unique environment of seabird colonies in the area, will it be possible to gather enough international support to fight for the plight of the Southern Ocean and its wildlife.

Tourism activities on New Island are also important for the reserve itself, as they provide a much needed and relatively predictable source of income that can be re-invested in infrastructure and management. Visits to New Island also assist the development of the island-wide tourist industry.

New Island was the first site in the Falkland Islands visited by eco-tourists. Ever since the start of land-based tourism operations in the summer of 1973, great care has been put into managing them in a sustainable and environmentally friendly way.

Today, land-based tourism on New Island has been largely discontinued due both to restrictions on access to the island by air, and on accommodation availability due to the Trust's committments to providing a research base on the island during the tourist season. However, the island remains one of the highlights for many cruise ship passengers who call at different locations around the Falklands.

New Island has maintained a policy of only allowing tourist ships of a certain size to land passengers on the reserve. The largest vessel visiting New Island has a capacity of approximately 160 passengers and this, based solely on past experience, appears acceptable in terms of environmental management.

In the 2005 season, which is representative of tourism activities in recent years, a total of 11 different vessels called at New Island, totalling 19 visits. Of these, some 16 involved New Island South. It is estimated from ships' passenger lists that approximately 1,535 passengers came ashore. The average number of persons landing on any one visit was 81. The average visit lasted 3.5 hours, with an average of 2 hours being spent at the Settlement Rookery.

The number of calls at New Island may rise, but it is important to recognise that Antarctica is their prime destination and the economics of operating these cruises may well reduce their visits to places like New Island. If on the other hand, visits to New Island are deemed excessive, the NICT as landowners would be in a position to limit the number of calls.

Zoning and Areas with Restrictions of Access or Use

A common sense rather than a dictatorial approach is made on the reserve, with researchers and visitors having free access to the whole of the island.

Ship-borne visitors are generally restricted to a few specific areas which were originally selected for their suitability in terms of low impact on wildlife, but also for their fair representation of the environment. Consideration was also given to the relative ease of access for such visits, where time is often a constraint.

All visitors are requested to abide by a small number of common sense rules. During short visits, normally from ships, small groups are accompanied by expedition guides or Reserve staff while walking ashore (the NICT's full Code of Practice for visitors can be viewed in Annex 10).
In addition to the rules laid out in this code, it is our policy not to allow any "hands-on" research in The Bowl area of the Settlement Rookery, and other no-go areas to field workers are designated as controls. Only non-invasive observation studies are made.
The Bowl was designated as the main area for tourist visits in the early 1970s. It was chosen for its suitability as a good observation point and one that has natural barriers. Research artefacts, ringed, or otherwise marked birds would, if present, potentially spoil the visitors' experience.

Photo above: Visitors to one of the reserve's Fur seal colonies in the 1970's. Fur seal are easily disturbed, but the nature of the site itself removes the need for signs and barriers, allowing visitors a completely natural wildlife experience whilst causing no disturbance to the animals

Monitoring Visitor Impact on the Environment

Most visitors to New Island visit The Bowl area of the Settlement Rookery. This area has been visited since 1973, and until 1995 was also an area used by researchers (as mentioned above, it is now restricted to observation-only research).
The Bowl's use for larger numbers of ship-borne visitors was based on the experience

gained from earlier studies. Visitors, researchers and residents, albeit in smaller numbers, had no detrimental effect on the three main species found breeding there, (Black-browed albatross, Rockhopper penguins and King Cormorants). Observations show that those birds nesting in The Bowl are generally much tamer than birds in areas which are not visited.

Photo above: Cruise ship passengers visiting The Bowl at the Settlement rookery.

Today, this area is an important "control" to gauge the effect of both tourists and researchers. In 2005 and 2006 comparisons were made between the breeding success of seabirds in the most often visited area with other, less disturbed parts of the Settlement colony (See Annex 4).

Other sites occasionally visited by tourists are the Fur seal colony, situated near Landsend Bluff, and seabird colonies at the North End. The Fur seal colony is situated at the base of a fairly severe cliff, with a good observation point at the top. Visitors have no means of access to the actual colony, making it virtually self-protecting (see photo opposite).

At the North End visitors do not enter colonies and are requested to keep to defined pathways, which skirt the colonies.

In 2005 a programme was initiated to monitor the erosion effects of visitors on the most often used paths. Such paths are used not only by visitors, but also by researchers, residents and, in some cases, vehicles. Although erosion needs to be monitored over long time frames before a definite conclusion can be reached, initial observations suggest that most of the areas regularly walked are well grassed. Where erosion occurs, vegetation generally recovers during the seven or so months when the reserve is closed for the winter. Such walks cover a very small part of the Reserve and are irrelevant compared with erosion on the island's vehicle track network.

Future Policy for Tourism on New Island

Presently, the level of tourism on New Island has no significant, measurable impact on the environment, either through erosion or through disturbance to seabirds and other fauna and flora. Although the potential exists for tourists to have an impact as a means of transport for invasive species, such potential seems to be reduced when compared to the frequent transportation of people and cargo to New Island related to non-tourist activities (e.g. research, supplies for residents and others).

More data on the present flora and invertebrate fauna of New Island, plus a basic monitoring programme to detect invasive species, might be advisable.

Given the low impact of tourism and considering its benefits, tourist activities at the present level are expected to proceed without major reservations.

Control of Introduced Animals and Plants

Even when introduced species seem to have reached an equilibrium with the local biodiversity, they might remain a potential hazard, should there be ecosystem changes driven, for example, by climate shifts. The removal of invasive species might allow the re-colonisation or recovery of some native taxa.

Ideally, all introduced taxa should be removed from New Island. However, in practice, there are many species, in particular plants and some mammals that cannot be successfully removed. This places a note of caution on any such plan (for further detail see: Possible Impact of Introduced Mammals and Plants, Pg.82).

Considerable success has already been achieved in removing horses, cattle, sheep, pigs and dogs. The removal of grazers has allowed a remarkable recovery of vegetation, notably of many native plants. Bird populations, in particular ground nesters, have increased and species which may originally have occurred on the island, have returned to breed. Erosion is no longer a major problem and water resources have increased due to re-vegetation.

Gorse continues to be the subject of control measures and a partial eradication programme has now been completed, (see Pg. 78). Gorse has a considerable aesthetic value and is part of the cultural landscape of the Falkland Islands. It also provides a nesting habitat for some bird species, even though this is shared with invasive species such as rabbits, rats, mice and cats.
On New Island it also appears to be an important habitat for the Green Spider *Araneus cinnabarinus*.

While there is no need to eradicate Gorse completely from the Settlement area, its development will continue to be contained.

Photo left: Gorse in flower

Preventing Further Introductions

New Island, like many other islands in the Falklands, has been a place of exploitation, refuge and place of human settlement since about 1774. Farming activities began in the late 1850s on New Island and probably resulted in the introduction of many non-native species of plants and animals seen today.

Unlike the very few pristine sites that remain in the Falkland Archipelago such as Beauchêne Island and Bird Island, New Island is not pristine. However, wherever practical, care continues to be taken to avoid the introduction of plants, insects and other animals.
Field scientists, as part of their study remit and a new initiative, are required to report on any new plant species appearing on the island and if found, to assist with eradication measures.

In relation to the possibility that visitors might bring seeds of invasive plants or other biota (Bergstrom & Chown 1999; Chown & Gaston 2000), observations in the area over the past many years, have failed to notice any introduced plant species that would have appeared and spread from the tourist areas.

Ship-based visitors generally make what are called "wet" landings. Brought ashore in Zodiacs, landings require visitors to first wade ashore in shallow sea water, which effectively cleans their boots. The design of these inflatable boats, loading and landing procedures, and distances from ship to shore, are all effective barriers for the introduction of rats or mice.

Photo below: Cruise ship passengers visiting New Island do so via Zodiacs, wading through shallow sea water before stepping ashore

New Island settlement

The Island's Infrastructure

The island's settlement and its infrastructure is in all respects the lifeline of the work that is carried out on the reserve. It still retains infrastructure in the form of buildings which date to early settlement, but since its establishment as a reserve in 1973, all new infrastructure has been designed around its work as a research centre.

The Settlement

The origins of the present settlement can be traced back to Captain Barnard's building, a rough stone shelter constructed in the years 1812-13. The regulating parameters for human settlement were to change very little from Barnard's time, when a secure anchorage, water, shelter from prevailing winds and fuel in the form of peat were essential for survival on such islands, or indeed anywhere else in the Falkland Islands.

The first settlers on New Island, nearly forty years after Barnard was marooned, would have noted the same essentials. It is most probable that the remains of his building were used as shelter and adapted for their own use by the Smith Brothers settlers in 1860. Mary Trehearne in her book "Falkland Heritage, A record of pioneer settlement" (1978), refers to the use of a building in 1868 which matches the form of Barnard's shelter. The present day settlement then developed from that site over the subsequent 150 years.

The Settlement is in all respects the lifeline of the reserve and the work carried out on the island. Without the essentials such as water supplies, power, communication systems, accommodation and a host of other facilities, which are often taken for granted in this modern age, the level of scientific and other research we see today would not exist on New Island.

There are presently three main houses, two smaller self-contained "A" frame chalets and a small fibreglass "Igloo" building forming the main settlement accommodation.

Two of these houses are pre 1972, the larger of the two is leased to T. Chater, until 2011, who resides there with his family. The remainder have been built specifically for the New Island Project in the years following. One of these buildings, "Prion House" is owned and retained by Ian Strange for his family.

Accommodation available for field personnel ranges from four to eight person capacity, depending on whether couples or single operatives are employed. Experience has shown that on such a remote island, accommodation has to allow individuals their own space and it is our policy to assist with this.

The Geoffrey C. Hughes Field Station

The reserve has good infrastructure in terms of buildings and other facilities. It has an excellent and large field station, the "Geoffrey C. Hughes Field Station" named after its benefactor. There is a large dry workplace where the preparation of specimens and equipment maintenance can be carried out. There is an office with a growing library which is an important aspect of this facility. A kitchen, dining area, bathroom and store room with a deep-freeze for keeping foodstuffs is provided. The second floor has a large room used for presentations and study groups which doubles up as a second office facility. On the same level there is large bedroom.

Outbuildings

A garage is used to house a Ford tractor plus a variety of other equipment. Due to costs and logistical difficulties in building on remote outlying islands such as New Island, most buildings erected after 1972 have been designed for dual purpose use.

A generator shed equipped with a Lister 7kw generator plus spares and equipment doubles up as a vehicle housing in winter, and also provides housing for a portable fire pump and hoses.

Electricity Supply/Power Systems

Since 1974 efforts have been made to harness natural energy using wind turbines and solar panels. In 2001 the New Island Trust, aware of the importance of reducing further the dependence on conventional fuels, but not qualifying under a Government scheme to aid the purchase of alternative energy systems offered to farms, invested in a new 2.5 kilowatt wind turbine, 48 volt battery bank and inverter. A purpose-built battery shed houses the battery bank, inverter and other electrical equipment.

This facility has transformed New Island's energy systems and it is now possible to offer a 24-hour power system, supporting appliances such as freezers, lighting and power tools etc. Only occasionally is there a need to use the backup 7kw generator during shortfalls in calm weather. Small solar panels are used for smaller energy supplies, topping up vehicle batteries and equipment in the field.

At the present time with careful use of the main storage batteries, the wind turbine system copes with the normal load expected from 4-10 personnel. However as research methodology moves towards the use of more electronic equipment, power requirements may change.

Photo below: A 2.5KW Proven Energy wind turbine provides clean energy. Also shown: the Field Station and outbuildings

Alternative Energy Sources

Sunshine levels are generally higher on New Island than in many places in the Islands and data on these levels is presently being collected through an automatic weather system. Depending on the results, a solar energy system could provide another alternative energy source. With the installation of a second 800 amp hour battery bank for use in summer, when power requirements are higher due to research activity, the facility would be well supplied with energy for years to come.

Heating

At the time of writing, heating systems run on gas, kerosene or diesel. Only rarely is wind power enough to produce any sizeable amount of electricity for heat. However, with 24-hour power it has been possible to install more efficient boilers, with a considerable saving in kerosene and diesel fuels.

Water Supplies

Water is a prime constituent of the island's management. With the present water supplies and spring flow, it is possible to support 4-10 personnel with confidence. In the short term it is possible to store sufficient water to allow a good standard in living facilities, with flush toilets, showers and laundry. This is above the water required for drinking and cooking, etc.

With careful control, the storage tanks can be topped up as required through the summer season from the one main spring. This takes into account that at the same time water continues to be available for wildlife. As the purpose behind the reserve is to preserve and protect this life, it would be neither prudent or right to be taking the total water supply for the needs of personnel.

It would be possible to increase the water holding capacity by building more storage tanks. The drilling of a bore hole to extract more water is an option to consider, especially as boring equipment is presently being used in the Falklands for mineral exploration.

Serious thought has even been given to installing a system whereby sea water might be used for the toilets. Extra water would allow the Trust to increase the number of personnel it might have on the island, but then other aspects, accommodation and power have to be considered.

Communications Systems

New Island has up-to-date telecommunications with a Micro-Wave Station operated by Cable & Wireless South Atlantic, which provides a good local and international telephone system, operating on a number of separate lines including fax and internet access.

The Micro-Wave Station is powered by solar panels. The New Island management carries out basic maintenance of the solar panels and batteries.

Automatic Weather Station

The operation of semi or fully automatic weather recording instruments has been a part of the New Island project for a number of years. Daily weather observations are also made, these being passed to the Falkland Islands Government Air Service. As the islands are subject to many micro weather patterns, the gathering of weather data to aid research on New Island is vital.

To improve and upgrade weather data, a new automatic weather station manufactured by Campbell Scientific was installed in early 2006 *(photo above)*.

The station registers wind speed, direction,

temperature, atmospheric pressure, sunshine levels and rainfall. A CR 510 data logger records information every hour and will record and store up to eight months of data.

Powered by solar energy, the station is designed to be linked to a communications system, such as the present micro wave station or satellite system, thus allowing information to be available worldwide.

Tracks and Transport Facilities

New Island has one main track running from the settlement in two main directions. To the south it goes to the airstrip *(photo right)* and to the north it goes to the North End Beach. From this main track a short spur on the southern section runs to a waste disposal area on the west cliffs. On the northern section of this main route, another short spur runs to a position close to the Settlement Colony also on the west cliffs. There are further tracks that go to the Fur seal colony and also towards Bold Hill.

The tracks are not "all weather" and although considerable sections are useable in wet conditions, there are sections which are difficult to use after a rainfall or in winter, due to their surface and steep nature.

Although difficult, due to essential use of the airstrip, it is policy to try and restrict the use of tracks in winter. It is also policy, gained from many years of experience, to employ finer tread tyres which have a less damaging effect on the island's fragile soils.

Attempts are continually being made to improve sections of the track but it is very doubtful if it could be made suitable in its entirety for all-weather conditions due to costs and the lack of suitable machinery. Ground transport is limited and restricted to functional vehicles, namely one Land Rover and one 4WD pick-up and a tractor, all needed for essential support operations. Most field work is carried out without the need for transport, although there is a need for a vehicle to carry passengers and freight to and from the airstrip, approximately 3.5 miles from the settlement. There is also a legal requirement for a vehicle to tow a fire tender for the airfield operations.

Jetty and Slipway

Refurbished under a Government scheme in October 2006, the island now has a good jetty and slipway. Situated at the settlement harbour, this very important facility allows the unloading of stores, materials and fuel drums, brought ashore by sea truck from local cargo vessels.

Airstrip

The airstrip is another very important facility, giving New Island an essential transport system for residents and researchers as well as providing carriage of mail and some freight. Without such a link, New Island could not function to the level it does.

The grass airstrip *(photo below)* is situated on the southern part of the island; it is a single strip with an alignment of 330 degrees. The Falkland Islands Government Air Service (FIGAS) operate into the strip on an "as required" basis but under restricted parameters. Operations are weather dependent, and the strip has a maximum passenger load of three passengers.

Strip maintenance is the responsibility of the island management who is also the licensee. The operation of the airstrip itself is not seen as an environmental impact problem, although the access track is responsible for some erosion and in parts is badly worn.

Infrastructure Controls in General

Vehicles

The development of New Island as an important research site, with associated infrastructure, has meant that vehicles have become an essential element in its work. However, as detailed in the sections related to tracks and ground transport, great care is taken to avoid excessive erosion and damage to tracks and even the choice of new vehicles is carefully considered.

The use of vehicles to reach research sites or for non-essential work is discouraged. It is a policy to restrict vehicle driving to the main tracks, except for a few infrequent exceptions linked to works on infrastructure, Gorse clearing, fence removal etc. Driving vehicles off the main tracks, especially by inexperienced drivers, can cause damage to vegetation and prion burrows. The recovery rate on New Island is very slow due to its relatively thin soil layers and low rainfall.

Removal of Fencing

When New Island was first taken over by NIPCO it had over 20 miles of sheep fencing. As part of the original management policy, fences were taken down, largely from an aesthetic point of view. A percentage of main fence posts were left, both as perches for birds and as identification for different areas.

Observations have shown that prions and other species are occasionally killed by entanglement with standing fences. All standing fences have already been removed on the southern half of the island and this will now continue on the recently acquired northern section.

Photo above: The late Ingrid Schenk, clearing up old fencing on the south reserve

Fire Control

The bright red patches of soil on parts of the island, which occasionally become exposed on the surface, are remnants of past fires. Some no doubt were caused by lightning, but some were deliberate as recorded by the captain of the whaler *Aurora* in 1820, when some of his men set fire to the Tussac to the north of Ship Harbour. Burning caused by lightning is recorded most years in the Islands and deliberate burning by farmers, especially on the mainland of East Falkland, is an annual procedure.

New Island is potentially at risk from lightning strikes and with its low rainfall and dense vegetation is perhaps more vulnerable than many other islands. The reality is that should a fire occur, there is very little that could be done. Prevention of fire, at least from any human source, is therefore paramount.
A strict no smoking policy exists on the island and all visitors, including tourist vessel passengers are informed of the dangers. Camping is not allowed in an effort to reduce the possibility of fire from an accident with camping stoves.
In certain circumstances, usually early in the season when the ground is still wet after winter rains and in very calm conditions, waste timbers and rubbish which cannot be disposed of in any other way, are burnt on open ground. Gorse bushes have, in the past, also been burnt, but extra care has to be taken.

A portable fire pump is owned by the Trust. This pump has sufficient hose to cover most of the settlement buildings, with the pump drawing water from the jetty. One of the disused fresh water storage tanks is kept full for use in an emergency. There are the required number of hand-operated extinguishers in all accommodation areas and essential buildings.

All new staff and researchers are made familiar with the fire fighting equipment and where possible taught how to operate it. It is policy that all longer term researchers have fire training on equipment used for the operation of the airstrip. Training is provided by the FIG Civil Aviation Department.

Waste Management

The disposal of all waste has been a management priority since the island was taken over in 1972/73. Several seasons were spent not only clearing hard waste such as corrugated sheeting, old drums, glass, rotting timbers and old buildings, but clearing the land of sheep and cattle carcasses, thus removing a food source for rodents.

Organic Waste
Organic waste is normally disposed of at sea, although poultry waste is not made available to scavengers such as skuas, Giant petrels and gulls, because of the possible risk of introducing avian disease to the island. New Island is 150 miles / 18 to 20 hours sailing time from the nearest official waste collection site. Shipping waste out is not practical and cost prohibitive, therefore we are obliged to dispose of our own waste.

Non-organic Waste
Non-organic waste is normally burnt inside old oil drums, or in a specially constructed incinerator, as conditions permit. Residue from burning is reduced as much as possible and is then disposed of into deep water where it is further broken down. Batteries or any other potentially toxic waste cannot be shipped out and are stored in a holding area until a suitable disposal system is found.

Sewage
In the past, sewage pipes and outlets have been run to the nearest point on the coast with the outfall going directly into the sea. The most recently built accommodation units have been fitted with sewage systems employing cess-pits, thus reducing potential food for rodents. It is planned to install cess-pits for the two remaining houses.

Beach Clean-Ups

Beach clean-ups were first started in the summer of 1972 and continue today. An annual sea-borne rubbish survey is normally carried out on one specific beach on the west side of the island. This is mainly the task of management, but also includes the help of field research staff and volunteers.

Maintaining a pristine coastal environment by clearing away sea-borne rubbish is one of the reserve's priorities. One particular area known to collect large amounts of debris is a gulch frequented by Sea Lions (above) - rubbish such as rope and fishing line are potential hazards to these animals
Opposite page: The crystal clear waters of the South End Beach

New Island Infrastructure

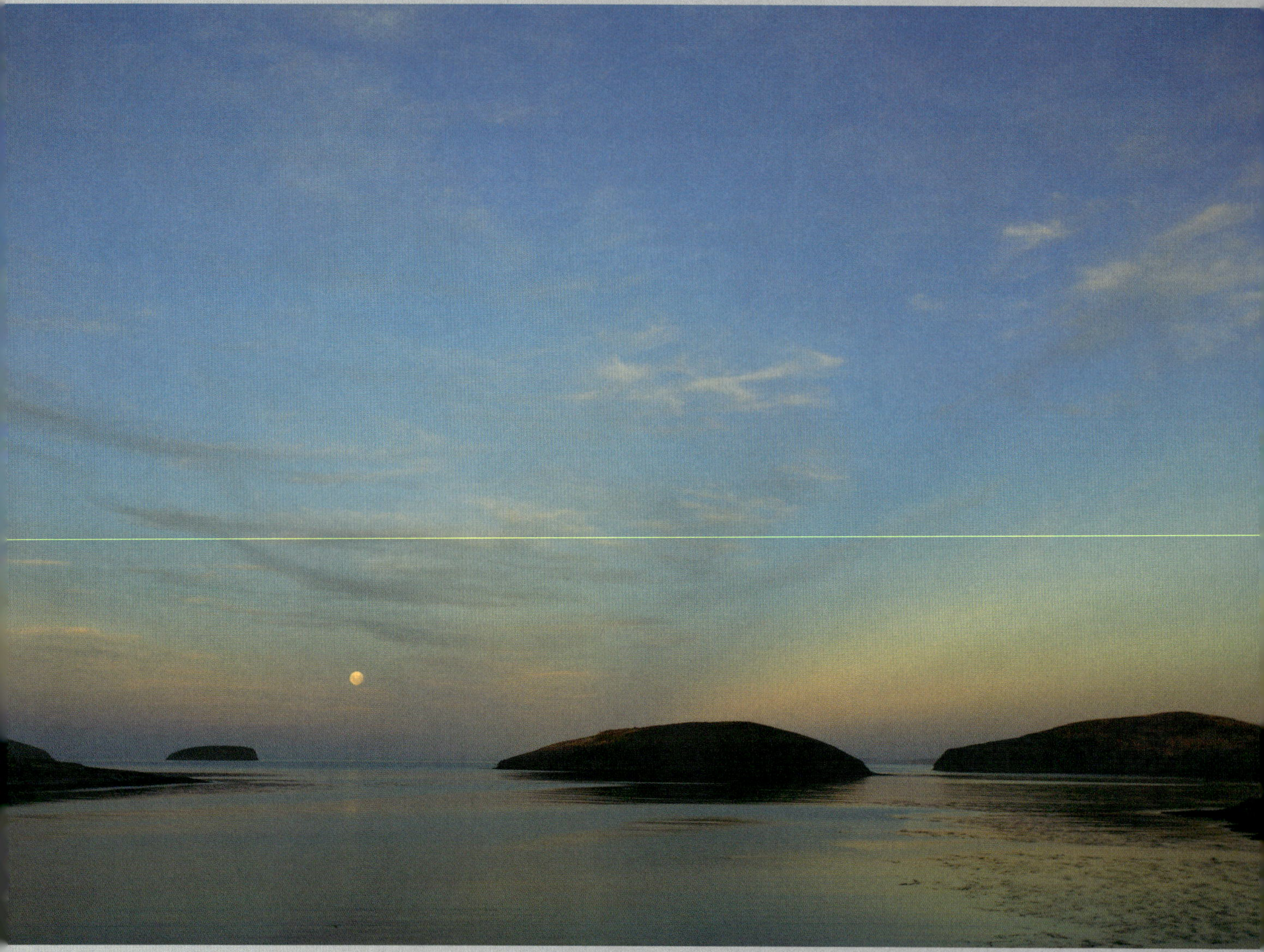

From the Founder of the New Island Conservation Trust
Ian J. Strange MBE

The success of the original New Island Project and what it has developed into today, can perhaps be measured by the numbers of researchers who continue to work here and sadly by the larger numbers who have to be turned away. The support given by the Falkland Islands Government for some of its projects, substantial support by The Overseas Environmental Program (OTEP) and that of private donors, are all indicators of its position and recognition as an important operation.

It is hoped that what is written in the preceding pages will document the many different aspects of the New Island reserve, from its past history, its spoliation by man over many decades and the development of the reserve; but that it will also serve as a valuable baseline.

In the future new ideals will surface and management plans may change, but the island's past, the mistakes as well as the achievements, must go down as historical fact. As discovered when this document was being written, no management plan for the present, or for the future, can ignore the past.

Photo opposite: The full moon rising over New Island's Settlement Harbour

Annex 1

Captain Charles Barnard's Building, New Island, 1813: A History

Written by Ian J. Strange, with extracts compiled from Barnard's original narrative

Introduction

In 1813 Captain Charles Barnard, while engaged in a sealing venture around the Falkland Islands with his brig *Nanina*, was marooned on New Island along with four of his men. The events occurred in the context of the war between America and England in 1812. After rescuing the survivors of the wreck of the British ship *Isabella* which had gone ashore on Speedwell Island, Barnard, an American from Nantucket, and his four men were left on New Island by the very men he had saved.

With his own vessel stolen, Barnard and his companions were left with only a few personal items, his dog and an open boat. For two years they survived on or about the island until eventually rescued. Barnard described his exploits in a book he published in 1829 ("Marooned - A Narrative of the Sufferings and Adventures of Captain Charles H. Barnard,1812-1816").

Barnard and his men constructed a rough stone building on New Island. Its exact position on the island was however unclear and for some years there was speculation on where his original camp site might have been. A lot of research and patience eventually led to us obtaining an original copy of Barnard's narrative and map.

The information that follows takes some of his accounts from his original writings and combines them with first hand knowledge of New Island to position his building accurately.

The Geographical Positioning of Barnard's Building

The narrative has a chart drawn by Barnard. It shows anchorages used by Barnard during his time in the Falkland Islands. Three anchorages are marked at New Island: one in South Harbour, one in Ship Harbour (in Barnard's time known as Coffin's Harbour) and Hooker's Harbour, (or Tigre Harbour; now referred to as Settlement Harbour). Barnard's chart does not show at which anchorage his house was built. However, his narrative gives a detailed description of his exploits on New Island. When these are analysed, it is possible, with knowledge and experience of the island's natural and physical environment, to identify the exact location of his camp site.

NEW ISLAND
Location Map of Barnard's Camp & Building

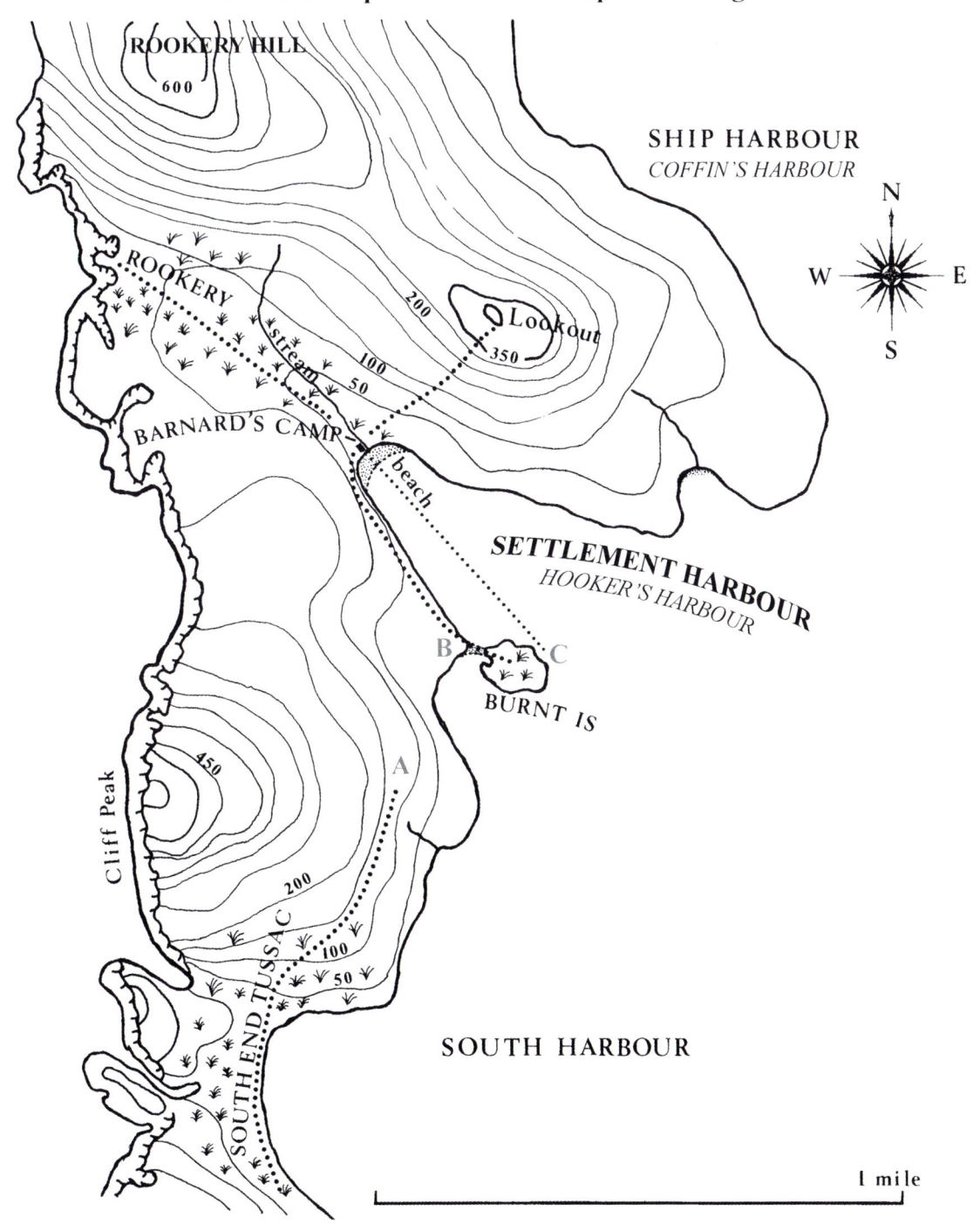

The map above shows an area of New Island from Rookery Hill, south, to the far end of the South End Tussac. Barnard's camp (and the location of the present Barnard Building) is shown at the head of Settlement Harbour, once known as Hooker's Harbour. Points A, B and C represent positions around the island to which Captain Barnard made reference in his narrative, "Marooned". These are described on the following pages, 112 & 113.

Photo opposite: Captain Barnard's Building as it is today. New Island settlement to the right, and the wreck of Protector III at the head of Settlement (Hooker's) Harbour

If we take first the location of the harbour, Barnard's narrative describes the north side of the harbour as being formed from a high hill. He frequently used this hill and wrote of his observatory on the top. He describes the Tussac having been burnt and the fire having caused the moor to develop large holes on this hillside, which is comparable with what we see today on Ferguson's Hill. His description of the beach and its peculiar tidal conditions identify this as the present Settlement Harbour beach, or as it is also known, The Protector Beach.

Barnard made a specific reference to Coffin's Harbour and makes a distinction between his camp site position and the former by writing *"I travelled over to this place"* which, with other descriptions, eliminates Coffin's Harbour (now Ship Harbour) as a possible site.

In another reference, Barnard describes a journey southward from his camp site:

"We passed round the mountain which makes the SW part of Hooker's Harbour and then descended, engaged in conversation to cross the valley. This valley is full of tushooks, which are higher than a man's head..."

This description leaves little doubt that the "mountain" is Cliff Peak, which shelters the SW side of the Settlement Harbour, (Hooker's Harbour). His journey round this "mountain" would then descend into a valley "full of tushooks", [Tussac Grass], an area we know as the South End Tussac.

A description of his return journey gives further confirmation:
"I returned through the tushooks and proceeded with expedition towards our camp. Having gone about a mile, and being half way round the mountain, I perceived the boat running out of the harbour".

Photo below: Captain Barnard's stone lookout shelter as it is today, atop Ferguson's Hill, overlooking Settlement (Hooker's) Harbour, Burnt Island cay, South Harbour and Beaver Island in the distance

Photo above: Burnt Island cay, at the mouth of Settlement Harbour, where Barnard and his men would have gone to collect peat

A route taken through the South End Tussac, to a point approximately half way round Cliff Peak is about one mile and would at that point allow Barnard to see his boat leaving the harbour (see map, point A).

In a further reference Barnard describes a southerly gale and a swell on a beach:
"The weather about the 10th (June), became very cold, and a severe storm commenced from the south, accompanied by squalls of snow, and continued until the next day.
While Ansel and myself were sitting by the fire, we thought we heard the voice of a man, and listened attentively, we heard it repeated. Running out we descried our boat on the beach, and the three men standing in the surf, and holding on to her, calling for help to haul her up. The wind was blowing in, and there was a considerable swell; but we got the things out, and dragged her above high water mark".
This description fits perfectly the conditions which can develop on the Settlement beach in such weather.

At the entrance and to the south side of the Settlement Harbour (Hooker's Harbour), there is a small islet or cay. This is accessible from the main island at low tide. Being the only islet with this feature attached to New Island, it is in itself a positive identification of the above harbour (see map, point B; and photo above).

"From a small key at the mouth of the harbour, well known by the name of Burnt Island"

"Our peat stack being consumed, we were obliged to bring peat from Burnt Island, which could be done only at low water, and was our heaviest duty..."
This small cay, also referred to as Peat Island by early whalers, lies half a mile from the beach where his camp was established. Carrying seal skin bags of peat from the islet would have been their "heaviest duty". Captain Weddell mentions taking supplies of peat from this islet and evidence exists today showing that the area was burnt many years ago, thus accounting for these earlier names.

There is then the question of locating the actual position of the building. An engraving in the original narrative illustrates from a seaboard position a sand beach with rocky beach areas each side. Just above the beach and to the left is Barnard's building. What can be described as tussac grass is shown going up the valley in the background and to the right.

The engraving, although perhaps not accurate in its detail and perspective, is a fair reconstruction of the Settlement Harbour sand beach as it appears today. In a further section of his writings, Barnard leaves another clue:

"There was a strong gale from the SSW, accompanied by showers of hail, on the 8 December. The tide was remarkably low, far beyond common low water mark. I walked out to almost where the brig had lain at anchor, but nothing but the sky and ocean met my inquisitive view. I was now employed at the walls of the house, which were about nine feet by seven, and more than three feet thick. While at work I was surprised at hearing a loud crack, like the breaking of a board; I looked towards my signal and register pole and saw that it was broken, with nothing in sight that could have done it. This to me was really unaccountable: I went to examine it, when I found beside it a large shag, lying dead, which had been flying down the valley to go a-fishing in the harbour, as many of them do every morning. They fly with great rapidity and cause a whistling in the air like a cannon ball passing near at hand. This one in his flight, came with such force against the topmast, which I had lashed to the head of the pole, as to carry it away, and cause his immediate death."

In certain wind conditions, particularly those from a southerly quarter, King Shags frequently fly down from the Settlement rookery as Barnard describes.

His narrative also helps to position the building:
"While Ansel and myself were sitting by the fire, we thought we heard the voice of a man"

We know from his writings that there was a southerly gale with surf breaking on the beach at this time, yet the voices of their companions were heard, suggesting the building had to be close to the beach.

Taking another extract we have further evidence of this:
"While cooking some eggs, to my astonishment, I perceived the boat coming round a point of rocks, about half a mile distant; the men landed on the beach at the mouth of the harbour. "

This extract may not appear very significant, until one is positioned at the site of the present building. The boat in question was returning from the direction of Beaver Island, which lies to the south. Had Barnard's building been positioned in any other place than at a very low elevation close to the sand beach, his angle of view would have been much greater. Any boat approaching from this general direction would have been seen long before turning the rocky point he describes *(see map, point C and sight line from the camp site; and photo opposite).*

A small freshwater stream runs past the present stone structure, emptying onto the sand beach approximately two metres from the northeast corner of the building. There are several references to this "neighbouring run of water". Seal skins were soaked and washed in it, but probably the most significant are Barnard's references to geese:

"I told Louder that we would twist some rope yarns into a cord about the size of a codline, make a slipknot in one end, lay it on the beach, and lead the other end into the door of the house, and when the geese lit on the beach, which several flocks did every day to drink from a run of freshwater that emptied on the beach, that we would catch them by means of the noose.- I soon had the satisfaction of catching the gander by the legs, and drawing him up to the house, with the others following him almost

Photo below: Beef & Coffin Islands, with Burnt Island cay in the foreground

Photo above: Barnard's building, at the head of Settlement (Hooker's) Harbour, ca. 1994

to the door."
Today, groups of geese still appear daily on the beach and come within two to three metres of the present building in order to drink from this source of fresh water.

Several references are made to the "rookery". Barnard's descriptions leave no doubt that he is referring to what we now know as the Settlement rookery. This is situated on the west side of the island and approached through a low valley leading up from Barnard's building, a distance of only half a mile. Barnard's narrative describes collecting the eggs of albatross:

"I went to the rookery, and brought to my hut during the day four loads of eggs".
For a period Barnard was deserted by his men and left alone on New Island. Later when they returned to him, he wrote:

"We continued busily engaged until the 15th, when by calculation, we had a hundred barrels, which were thought to be a sufficient supply."
Collecting such a quantity of eggs in the time Barnard quotes would have been a relatively simple task from this particular rookery, but a difficult one from any other rookery, the nearest being three miles away over rough terrain.

The Building

With the possibility of having to remain on New Island for some time, Barnard decided to build a more substantial shelter:
"I now determined to work steadily at building a stone house, with a fire place, and endeavour to get a sufficient number of seal skins to cover the roof."

His initial "hut" had been of Tussac grass from the pedestals of Tussac grass growing close to the beach.

Later on he wrote:
"I was now employed at the walls of the house, which were about nine feet by seven, and more than three feet thick."

This building was constructed while Barnard was on his own. With the return of his other men, a larger shelter was required.

Barnard wrote:

"In three days we completed the walls which were from three to four feet thick, and five in height. But we had the most difficult part yet to accomplish, which was to make the roof, as we had not been able to procure drift wood enough for the rafters; but we luckily substituted the ribs of a whale, which we found on the beach. After the top was prepared in the best manner which our scanty means permitted for thatching, we pulled the longest tushook straw we could find, and secured it with old rope yarns, brought from the wreck for that purpose; and succeeded in making a thatch resembling that with which farmers cover their barns."

Barnard's narrative does not say if the building's floor area was extended from his initial stone structure, but does go on to mention that a bank of earth was raised around the house, against the walls to the top and sloping off six or eight feet.

One winter was spent in this building and, probably fearful of yet another, the decision was made in the spring to enlarge this:

"On the 20th October we began to take down one end of our house, extended the walls eighteen or twenty feet further, and then erected the gable end as before, intending to enclose it all under one roof. We secured the end of the ridge pole, so as to keep the old apartment under cover. The new wall was much better than the old, as we had laid the stones in a sticky blue clay, which we procured from under the sand, at a depth of about eighteen inches. The walls and the greater part of the roof were completed, when a stop was put to our further progress by the want of laths.
I concluded that Louder and Albrook should go to Swan Island [Weddell Island] for hogs, and likewise for some drift wood that we had seen at Loop's Head. We departed, leaving Ansel and Green to gather long tushook straw for thatching."

From this, a fairly accurate picture may be drawn of Barnard's final building. His measurements may not have been precise, but it is evident that the building was substantial. In length it was 25 to 29 feet and 7 to 9 feet wide. The height 5 feet, with walls 3 to 4 feet thick.

How skilled these men were at building is not recorded. However, it is known that apart from a hatchet made from an old adze, a large pocket knife and pieces of iron hoop, they had no tools. The walls therefore had to be built of rough uncut stones procured from the surface rather than quarried. The present Settlement beach presented the ideal site for this material and the only one where such a quantity of stone is available nearby.

Another important consideration is that these men were building a shelter for what they hoped would be only short-term use. The site they chose was functional, it offered protection from the prevailing weather, fresh water and was close to where they could haul up and guard their boat, their most important possession.

The Pre-Restoration Days of the Barnard Building

Prior to the building's restoration there stood on the site, as today, a fairly large rough stone and timber building. It had sawn timber roof trusses, supported in places by old ship's timbers of huge proportions. The actual roof covering was corrugated iron sheeting and beneath this a canvas covering on boards. Four of the main walls are well over six feet in height, some with corners of yellow brick. These walls are dry stone and clay and vary in thickness from approximately 22 to 38 inches. One of the walls has three arched windows with small panes of glass. There were four separate door openings into the building, two clearly for sheep work. The interior floor varies: parts were of sand and peat mix; a small area had been boarded as a shearing floor; and some areas were concreted. It is quite obvious that over the last 180 years the original building has been added to in order to suit the activities of various settlers.

There is no evidence to suggest it was used for long term accommodation, but it could have been used as living quarters and storehouse for whalers and sealers and probably by some of the earlier settlers on the island (see Early History: Crown Land Leases, Pg. 15).

There is evidence that it was used as a trying-out place, possibly for penguin and seal oil, later for beef and mutton tallow and as a shearing shed. Some 35 years ago it was still being used as a cow shed and killing house.

Exactly how much of Barnard's original building now forms the present stone work is not clear, but the existing south wall fits his description well. Five feet high, nearly three feet thick and over twenty feet long, it is built of relatively small undressed rocks. Some parts are dry stone, some bound with clay and much of its outside length backed by soil. During recent reconstruction work, one wall with a wide base has been discovered laid simply on deep soft sand. Whoever built in this manner was not considering any permanent structure. This might well be another part of Barnard's original "house".

Photo above: The Barnard Building in 1987

Present Day Restoration

Serious attempts at restoration of the building were first made in 1995 when parts of the north wall cracked and a section fell away. With a real danger that the main part would also fall, work commenced on clearing the collapsed section. At this stage it was discovered the walls had been laid on pure sand, in parts nearly a metre deep. Section by section the unstable ground was dug out and replaced with a concrete slab foundation and the stone walls replaced.

Apart from the original walls, all the additional sections which had been added at different times were laid with clay. Very small corner sections were laid with a rough shell lime and sand mix. For practical reasons, a cement mix was used to rebuild stone walls that had collapsed or had to be taken down and rebuilt. Large sections of wall which remained sound and stable were left as originally built.

In the process of clearing the foundations, considerable numbers of rough handmade bricks were discovered. The origin of these is still unknown and under investigation. One possibility being researched is that the bricks were originally used on early whalers, initially as ballast when

Photo opposite: The Barnard Building in 1975

en route south from places like Nantucket. Such bricks were then used for building try works, eventually being discarded when the vessels returned north with their cargoes of oil. These bricks now form the restored arched window cavities in the present building.

In the summer of 1999 the decision was made to replace the old and fast disintegrating corrugated iron sheeting on the building. With the help of a generous donation from the family of the late Bertha Dodge, who edited and wrote sections of Barnard's narrative "Marooned", a new roof covering was put on the building. In an effort to retain as much as possible of the dated interior, the old roof trusses were retained. Only months later, in what was generally accepted as a very unusual weather pattern, the complete roof with its trusses, was ripped off the walls. With only an automatic weather station as witness to the event, all that can be said is that the winds were from the southeast, persisted for some days, and that the highest gust recorded was 132 mph.

From the evidence left behind, one can only surmise at the strength of the winds. One complete half section of roof had flipped over and lay to one side of the building. This was intact, complete with its trusses and with hardly a scratch on its new sheeting. The much larger half section of roof had been taken close to 100 metres up the valley, with parts of the trusses speared into the ground en route. Supporting part of the interior of the roof horizontally was a ship's mast. Nearly forty feet in length and with a base diameter of some 10 to 12 inches, the mast had been snapped into four pieces and tossed outside the building. Every holding down strap which had been cemented into the stone walls, folded over the roof trusses and nailed, were still firmly cemented into the walls, but now all were stretched upright.

In September 2005 restoration was started, made possible by funds from the Overseas Territories Environmental Programme (OTEP). In the summer of 2006, restoration was finally completed and the building, with its unique historical importance and connections with the North American whaling and sealing industries, will remain an important historical landmark.

As the Captain Charles Barnard Museum and Visitor Centre, it will offer those who pass through its doors an insight into the past exploits of these industries, but just as important, it will show the present day work of scientific study and conservation of the life that was the basis of this past exploitation.

Photos - opposite page:
(Top) The restoration of the Barnard Building was started in September 2005 by Ian Strange & Dan Birch, with the clearing of turf and old flooring from the interior of the structure.
(Center) All the materials for the roof of the building had to be brought in by boat and carried ashore to the building site.
(Below) Ian Stewart, John Jaffray & Ian Strange placing the main support beams for the roof.

Photos - this page:
(Top) The completed building in its scenic location with the wreck of Protector III
(Center) The main doors to the Captain Barnard Memorial Museum & Visitors Centre
(Below) The interior of the building now houses historical artefacts such as these cart wheels and a 1935 Kongsberg whaling gun and harpoons

Black-browed Albatross on New Island's west cliffs

Annex 2

Conservation and Environmental Monitoring Projects: New Island, 2006 – 2011

1. Control of Gorse *Ulex europaeus*

Objective:
To destroy all patches of Gorse occurring away from the Settlement area and contain the spread of the species in the Settlement area by some 50%.

Justification:
Gorse is an invasive species, introduced from Europe, that forms monospecific stands. Although Gorse in the Falkland Islands does not have the rampant growth compared, for example, with New Zealand, it has been identified as providing a breeding habitat for invasive mammals on New Island, including mice, rats, cats and rabbits. However, the complete eradication of Gorse would not be practical, nor desirable, as it also provides shelter and a breeding habitat for birds, especially thrushes, siskins, Turkey vultures and Steamer duck.

Actions:
There are a number of gorse patches away from the Settlement that have been identified and mapped when producing the current Management Plan. All these patches are to be completely destroyed. In the Settlement, action will be taken to avoid any further spread of Gorse.

Funding and timing:
Gorse clearance is presently being carried out and comes under part of the OTEP funds for the implementation of the Management Plan in 2006/07.

2. Dismantlement of Fences

Objective:
To remove all remaining fences from New Island.

Justification:
There were some 20 miles of fences on the island in 1972. These had been erected to assist the management of sheep and cattle. Serving no purpose on New Island South, fences were gradually removed for aesthetic reasons and eventually cleared in 2006. They were also considered a hazard to night flying petrels, particularly Thin-billed prions, and a danger to Magellan penguins.

Action:
Dismantle remaining fences on the newly acquired northern section of New Island. Leave a percentage of posts as bird perches and as identification of original grazing areas.

Funding and timing:
The dismantlement of all fences on New Island South was completed in 2004/05 and 2005/06 under the funding of an OTEP project. Further work will be carried out in 2006/07, on New Island North, still under the funding from OTEP. There will be a need to continue such work beyond 2006/07.

3. Thin-billed Prions: Monitoring of Population and Breeding Performance

Objectives:
To monitor the breeding success of prions on New Island and to identify factors affecting population trends.

Justification:
New Island is home to largest known colony of this species. A long-term dataset using consistent methodology started in 2003, and some additional data are available from 1980 and 1998-2001. This is currently the only detailed study of this species in the South Atlantic.

Action:
To monitor parameters of provisioning and breeding success. Provisioning is monitored using daily chick weights, corrected for metabolic weight loss (see Quillfeldt et al. 2003 ff.), and additionally adults are detected in the colony using radiotelemetry. From the latter, foraging trip

durations can be determined.

To relate parameters of provisioning and breeding success to climatic parameters from the local scale (eg. winds), over regional oceanographic conditions (such as sea surface temperature) to global processes (e.g. El Niño Southern Oscillation).

To monitor diet, the use of different methods (e.g. regurgitates, stable isotope methods and fatty acid signatures) are currently being assessed.

To monitor movements away from the colony, stable isotopes of tissues representing diet during the breeding and interbreeding period (like chick and adult feather samples) are used. This should be continued through a number of breeding seasons to assess interannual variability.

To gain insights into mechanisms of the control of provisioning, the behavioral interactions of chicks and adults are monitored simultaneously (e.g. begging and feeding rates). These studies are used to evaluate how adult survival is balanced against investment into reproduction. In connection with this, hormonal levels, such as the avian "stress hormone" corticosterone, are also monitored.

To gain insights into mechanisms and consequences of flexible growth, as this will allow us in the long term to evaluate which consequences provisioning rates have on the future of the chick (survival to breeding and sublethal effects such as immune status).

Funding and timing:
Funding for the 2003-2011 has been secured through Deutsche Forschungsgemeinschaft, Germany (Emmy Noether Programme, Grants Qu148-1ff to Dr. Petra Quillfeldt).
In addition, support for stable isotope analyses have come from OTEP and NERC (UK).
Some additional funding may need to be sought for replacement of equipment etc.

4. Population Dynamics and Foraging Ecology of Black-browed Albatross

Objectives:
To monitor the albatross population on New Island and to identify the factors affecting population trends.

Justification:
The Black-browed albatross is considered a globally endangered species. They are still abundant in the Falklands, their main stronghold, and hence they can also be used for monitoring of the marine environment. The population dynamics study started in 2003 and currently under way on New Island is one of only two in the whole of the South Atlantic (the other is on Bird Island, South Georgia).

The long-term continuation of this study has recently been identified as of High Priority in the Recommendations included in the Proceedings of the International ACAP Meeting that took place in Stanley in March 2006 (published as "Albatross and petrels in the South Atlantic: Priorities and Conservation").

Besides the simple monitoring of population parameters, data should be gathered on the level of interaction and dependency of this population on food resources provided by fishing vessels.

Action:
To continue with the annual collection of demographic data (such as population size, adult survival, breeding success and juvenile recruitment).

To gather data on population size through aerial surveys.

To gather data on the diet and individual feeding specializations (using stable isotopes), and relate such information to demography. More data should be collected on the foraging locations of these birds, but this could also be included under Project 5.

Funding and timing:
Funding has already been secured (OTEP, Portuguese Science Funds and University of

Belfast) for the 2006/07 season (except for aerial surveys) and for part of the 2007/08 field and laboratory work.
Population monitoring should continue annually until 2011 and beyond, and funds need to be sought for this purpose.

5. Supporting the creation of a Marine Protected Area off West Falkland

Objective:
To gather knowledge needed to support the case for the creation of a Marine Protected Area covering key ocean sectors in West Falkland and to develop or support initiatives aiming at creating such an area. Proposals for the creation of a Marine Reserve were presented to the Falkland Islands Government by Ian Strange in 1999, 2002 and 2005.

Justification:
Many of the most important seabird and seal colonies of the Falklands are located in the westernmost sectors of the Falkland Islands, including the Jason Island chain, the New Island group, Bird Island and the Weddell Island group; most of which are reserves. This is an indication of the existence of an area of particularly rich marine life.

The area proposed is presently of low development potential from activities such as fisheries and oil exploration, but new interests in aquaculture could be a threat. It is also an area of exceptional value for the development of sustainable development initiatives, such as eco-tourism.
The main ecological values of New Island are linked to its seabird and seal colonies. The New Island Reserve only protects the breeding grounds of these animals and birds, but has no direct influence on their foraging grounds. Only by lobbying for a more effective and long-term protection of such foraging grounds will New Island be able to fully ensure the conservation of its natural heritage.

Information is needed on the biodiversity values of the marine area around West Falkland. Further information on the foraging grounds of seals and seabirds, including those reproducing on New Island, is also needed. The NICT is however fairly well advanced in their knowledge of the foraging grounds of penguins. (See "Applying ecology to conservation: Tracking breeding penguins at New Island South reserve, Falkland Islands", Boersma, Stokes & Strange, 2002).

Action:
To raise funds so that the following actions can be carried out:
(a) compile all the available information on the foraging grounds of seabirds and seals reproducing West of the Falklands, including oceanographic and biological data for the sector;
(b) prepare a further more detailed proposal, with a plan for the creation of a marine protected area;
(c) to continue lobbying for the creation of such a protected area.

Funding and timing:
Funding has not been secured towards this aim, but possibilities should be considered such as developing a partnership with other national and international NGOs (Falklands Conservation, Wildlife Conservation Society and SubAntarctic Foundation for Ecosystems Research [SAFER]), etc. to raise funds for field studies, for the compilation of all the available data and for lobbying activities.

Photo: Falkland Skua & chick

Annex 3

National Government Policies and International Commitments: Relevance of the Present Environmental Management Plan

Conservation & Biodiversity Strategy Action Plan: Falkland Islands

The present plan contributes to the implementation of the draft Falkland Islands Government "Conservation & Biodiversity Strategy Action Plan", in the following priority areas:

- **Sustainable use of resources:** Promoting sustainable tourism.

- **Gaining a better understanding of the Falkland Islands' natural environment:** Improving the current biodiversity inventory, studies of interactions with invasive species, monitoring the population dynamics of globally threatened species, improving visitor facilities and documentation that can be used for local education.

- **Improving the natural environment of the Falkland Islands through targeted action on the ground:** Control of invasive species, where it is proved appropriate, by assisting the management of this National Nature Reserve.

Environmental Charter of the Falkland Islands

The successful management of the reserve will contribute to the implementation of the Environmental Charter of the Falkland Islands by supporting the Falkland Islands Government to fulfill the following commitments:

- "Ensuring the protection and restoration of key habitats, species and landscape features through legislation and appropriate management structures and mechanisms, including a protected areas policy, and attempting the control and eradication of invasive species."

- "Implement effectively obligations under the Multilateral Environmental Agreements already extended to the Falkland Islands and work towards the extension of other relevant agreements, where appropriate."

- "Review the range, quality and availability of baseline data for natural resources and biodiversity."

- "Encourage teaching within schools to promote the value of our local environment (natural and built) and to explain its role within the regional and global environment."

- "Promote publications that spread awareness of the special features of the environment in the Falkland Islands; promote within the Falkland Islands the guiding principles set out above."

Convention on Biological Diversity

The sound environmental management of the New Island Reserve will help FIG meet future obligations under the Convention on Biological Diversity. The following is a brief review of the Convention's Articles:

- Identification and monitoring of biodiversity with attention to those requiring urgent conservation measures.

- Establish a system of protected areas. Develop guidelines for the management of protected areas, manage biological resources, rehabilitate and restore degraded ecosystems, control or eradicate those alien species that threaten ecosystems.

- Adopt measures relating to the use of biological resources to avoid or minimize adverse impacts on biological diversity.

- Promote and encourage research that contributes to the conservation and sustainable use of biological diversity.

- Public education and awareness.

Convention on Migratory Species & Agreement on the Conservation of Albatross and Petrels (ACAP)

The environmental management and research on the New Island Reserve also helps FIG meet obligations under the Convention on Migratory Species, more specifically under the Agreement on the Conservation of Albatrosses and Petrels (ACAP), through the research and monitoring of Black-browed Albatross and White-Chinned Petrel populations, and the study and monitoring of the possible impacts of introduced predatory mammals.

• **General conservation measures of ACAP:**
Initiate or support research into the effective conservation of albatrosses and petrels. Develop and maintain programmes to raise awareness and understanding of albatross and petrel conservation issues. Exchange information and results from albatross and petrel, and other relevant conservation programmes.

• **Capacity building of ACAP:**
Assistance to be provided to some Range States, including through research, training or monitoring for implementation of conservation measures for albatrosses and petrels and their habitats. For the management of those habitats as well as for the establishment or improvement of scientific and administrative institutions for the implementation of this Agreement.

Photo above: Black-browed Albatross at New Island's Settlement Rookery

Annex 4

An assessment of the possible impact of disturbance caused by tourists on the New Island South Reserve seabird colonies

Dr Paulo Catry, Rafael Matias & Riek van Noordwijk

Ship based tourists visit three sites on New Island, the main one being a small section of the Settlement Rookery called "The Bowl". During such visits, they follow well marked natural pathways which come close to nests of the following species: Black-browed albatross *Thalassarche melanophrys*, King cormorant *Phalacrocorax atriceps* and Rockhopper penguin *Eudyptes chrysocome*.

In 2004 and 2005 regular observations were made during tourist visits to qualitatively assess their behaviour and try to observe any negative interactions with the birds. Furthermore, breeding success was quantified by counting the number of nests where an egg had been laid and, later on, by counting nearly-fledged chicks.

Within The Bowl, nests or sub-colonies to which tourists have a direct close access were distinguished from more distant ones. We also monitored the breeding success of more distant sub-colonies, far from the areas visited by tourists.

Results shown in Tables 1-4 show that, in line with other ongoing studies, there are relatively important differences in breeding success among sub-colonies. Such differences are not consistent from one year to the next, and we believe they are caused by differential predation by a few specialist skuas and Striated caracaras, as well as from some localised diseases that seem to affect albatrosses at this site. In any case, there is no evidence for a reduced breeding success in the more intensively visited areas of the tourist site. On the contrary, even within The Bowl, Black-browed albatross nests more removed from the tourist paths had a lower breeding success than the ones with a more direct interaction with visitors (e.g. Table 2). Such results are not surprising, particularly if one considers the fact that we have never observed situations of temporary nest abandonment during tourist visits nor any successful predation attempts apparently linked to the presence of visitors.

Results for Rockhopper penguins (Table 3) also show significant differences between colonies, but no clear relationship with the level of tourist visitation.

Sub-colonies where tourists have close access to nests included the one site with the highest recorded breeding success, but also another two with respectively intermediate and low success in the 2004 season.

In the 2005 season, we obtained data on breeding success by counting nests after the end of egg-laying and then counting chicks just before fledging in two discrete subcolonies. The number of chicks raised per nest was not much lower on the most visited sub-colony in the Bowl area (0.96 chicks per nest, n = 118) than on a remote site with virtually no disturbance (1.06 chicks per nest, n = 104).

Data obtained for King Cormorants (Table 4) indicated a slightly higher breeding success in the tourist areas, again suggesting no negative impact from visitors.

It must be recognized that, due to the high spatial variability in breeding success of albatrosses, cormorants and penguins at this site, it would be particularly difficult to detect any mild impact of tourists on breeding success.
However, it is absolutely clear that, if such impact exists (and we have no evidence that it does), it must be very light indeed and no more than the impact by field scientists. Furthermore, only a tiny proportion of the seabirds nesting in the rookery area ever come into close contact with tourists, and even if visitors had a moderate impact on the breeding success at such plots, the overall success of the colony would remain virtually the same.

Table 1
Breeding success (number of chicks on 1st March per egg laid) of Black-browed albatross at different colonies on New Island. The Bowl is the main tourist area, while the control plot is never visited by tourists and only very rarely by researchers.

Year	"The Bowl"	Control
2004/05	54.1% (n=181)	52.1% (n=73)
2005/06	44.4% (n=169)	64.1% (n=64)

Table 2
Breeding success of Black-browed albatross in different areas of The Bowl. Tourists come within close reach of the albatross nests in area A, but less so in area B.

Year	"The Bowl" A	"The Bowl" B
2004/05	58.0% (n=69)	51.8% (n=112)
2005/06	51.2% (n=64)	40.0% (n=105)

Table 3
Breeding performance (number of chicks raised to the start of the creching period) of Rockhopper penguins in different sub-colonies of the Rookery in 2004/05, in relation to the regular presence of tourists.

Sub-colony	N	Chicks raised to end of brooding	Tourist presence
1	22	0.73	Close
2	26	0.81	Distant
3	23	0.48	Close
4	22	0.91	Distant
5	24	0.96	Distant
6	42	0.98	Close
7	34	0.41	None
8	35	0.97	None
9	24	0.71	None
10	26	0.65	None
11	8	0.88	None

Table 4
Breeding success of King Cormorants (mean ± SD number of chicks raised until creching/fledging per nest with eggs) on different colonies on New Island. The Bowl is the main tourist area, while the control plot is never visited by tourists.

Year	"The Bowl"	Control
2005/06	2.03 ± 0.84 (n=31)	1.76 ± 0.90 (n=58)

Annex 5

Black-Browed albatross *Thalassarche melanophris* Population Census at New Island South, Falkland Islands
September-October 2004, September 2006 and Population Increase Trends from 1977 to 2007
Ian J Strange

The Black-browed albatross *Thalassarche melanophris* is found all around the southern oceans between 25° and 60°S. Black-browed albatross form three distinct genetic groups: Falklands, Diego Ramirez/South Georgia/Kerguelen, and Campbell Island (Burg and Croxall, 2001). The species was recently re-assessed and given a conservation status of Endangered on the IUCN Red List for 2004 (IUCN, 2004). Decreases in breeding populations have been reported and are largely attributed to bycatch in long-line fisheries (Croxall and Gales, 1998; Gales, 1998; Tickell, 2000; Woehler et al., 2001). The Falkland Islands hold over 60% of the global population and are the most important breeding site in the world for this species. A 25% fall in population over the last 20 years, at colonies in the Falkland Islands, has been reported (IUCN, 2002).

The aim of the present study is to present results of recent surveys of the population of Black-browed albatross at the New Island South Nature Reserve in the West Falklands, together with a long-term data set.

Abstract

The aim of this study was to present results of two recent surveys of the population of Black-browed albatross (*Thalassarche melanophris*) at the New Island South Nature Reserve in the West Falklands.

Counts of adults returning to the colonies in late September-early October were conducted in the field and from aerial photography. Both methods gave comparable results.

The total count of prospective breeding pairs in 2004 was 3,324 pairs on the West Cliffs (6.9% annual increase compared with counts in 2000) and 1,890 pairs in the Settlement Rookery for the 2004 census (similar to counts in 2000). The 2006 census produced a count of 4,323 for the West Cliffs (23% increase over the 2004 count) and 2,001 pairs in the Settlement Rookery, an increase of 5.5% over the 2004 census).

One part of the population, known as the Settlement Colony, has been monitored with consistent methodology since 1977 and the present data describe the increase in the population of 100.5% over 29 years (an average of 3.5% per annum).

Additional census data from other populations in the area surrounding New Island are also presented, showing increases in several populations of albatross and Southern Giant petrel *Macronectes giganteus*. Possible reasons for these increases and implications for monitoring are discussed.

Methods

The study was carried out at New Island (51° 43' S, 061° 17'W), Falkland Islands (Fig. 1 and 2), between 1977 and 2006. New Island is one of the westernmost islands in the Falkland Islands, adjacent to the rich waters of the Falkland Current (Fig. 2).

Since 1977, fifteen annual counts of the breeding population of Black-browed Albatross at the Settlement Rookery (Fig. 1) have been made. Surveys were carried out between late September and early October when birds first return and commence egg laying. Three surveys (2000, 2004 and 2006) are reported on; these were carried out by aerial photography of birds colonizing the west coast cliffs of the island (Fig. 1 and 4). Additionally, a ground count was carried out in September-October 2004 and 2006 (see below for details).

The main criteria for selecting the period for the surveys are as follows:
1. The first looks at the population of potential breeders i.e. birds of adult age, which are

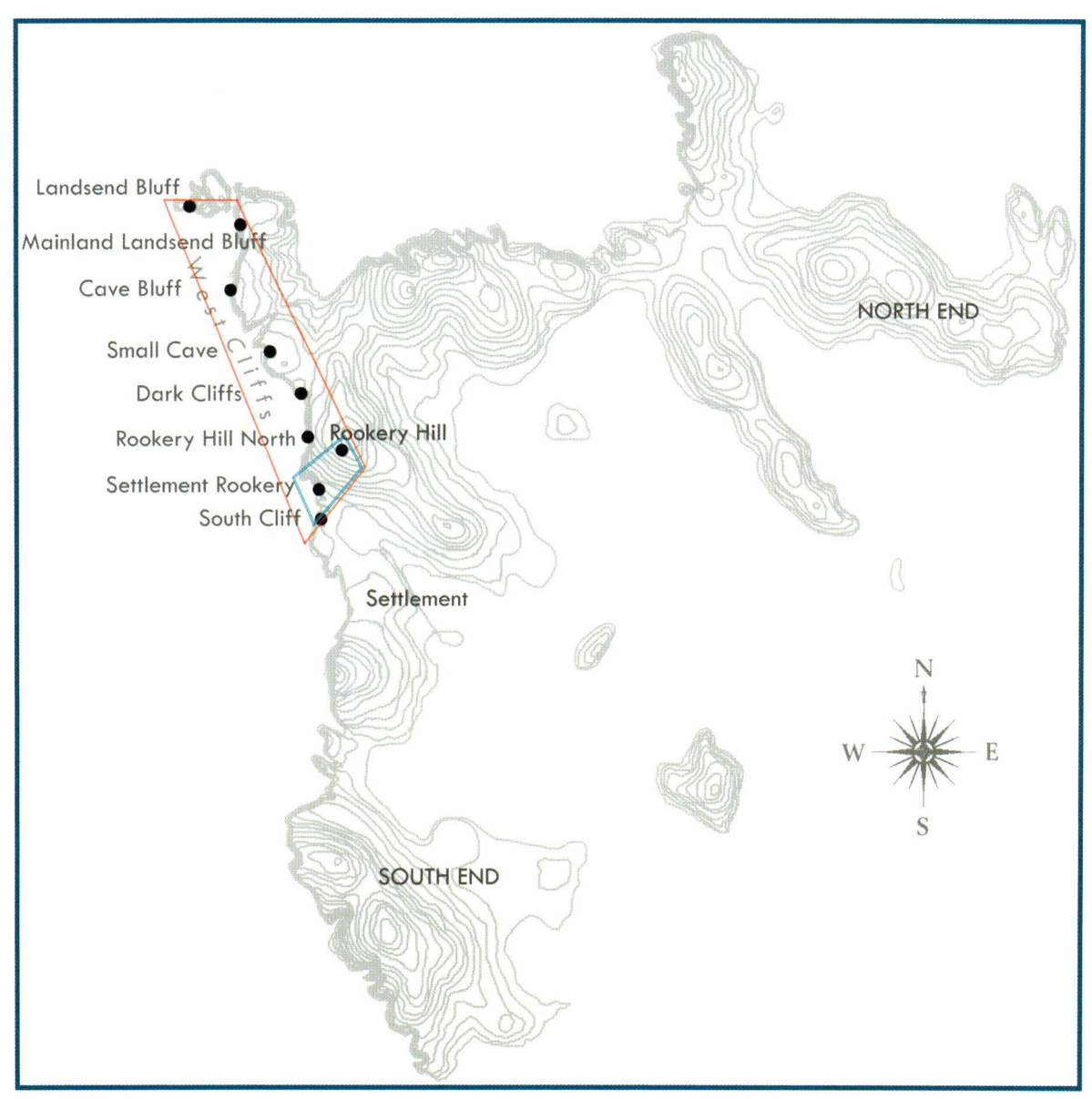

Fig. 1: *Map of New Island showing areas surveyed. Areas within the red box were surveyed using aerial methods; Areas within the blue box were surveyed using a combination of both aerial and ground methods*

returning to breed and birds appearing as first time breeders. This method gives an important base line for the number of adult birds returning to the New Island South colonies each year. From these figures it is then possible to look at other stages in breeding and establish rates of the number of birds laying, hatching and chicks fledging.

2. On the Settlement Rookery, Black-browed albatross nest with larger numbers of Rockhopper penguins *Eudyptes chrysocome* and King cormorants *Phalacrocorax (atriceps) albiventer*. Such mixed colonies are found at the majority of other sites in the Falklands. Surveys of individual species become very difficult when all these are nesting together, with the result that counts are subject to error. As the albatross return and commence breeding first, surveys of this species are made in late September through the second week in October. The Black-browed albatross on New Island usually commence egg laying in the last days of September into early October, coinciding with the return of the first male Rockhopper penguins. Taking these factors into account, the optimum period for counting breeding pairs of albatross on the island is between 26 September and 9 October.

The Settlement Rookery covers an area of approximately 1km². A large proportion of the Settlement Rookery is situated on south and southwest facing slopes of Rookery Hill between the 100 to 400 foot contours. Many of the albatross on these slopes tend to form relatively small compact colonies in well-defined areas. Others are situated on cliffs, which form the coastal fringe of this area (Fig. 4). Here nests are generally more scattered and on ledges or steep slopes. The south and southwest facing areas are clearly defined by prominent landmarks and offer good census sites. A smaller breeding area referred to as "The Bowl", but part of the Settlement Rookery, lies on a north-facing slope in a good location for surveying albatross. In 1986 a new colony of some twenty birds was noted on the western slopes of South Cliff. From this date birds were surveyed and added to the total for the Settlement Rookery.

Ground Counts

The large form, distinctive white plumage and nesting habits of Black-browed albatross make direct counting relatively easy in accessible areas, especially before the return of other species to this mixed colony. Counting is carried out from survey points, identified by weather-resistant hardwood stakes, which have clear views of the colonies. Counts are made visually, using detailed site maps of the area to identify individual colonies. Counts are backed up with photographs, which are also used to register changes in the development of vegetation. Where small groups of albatross are partly obscured by dense Tussac grass *Parodiochloa flabellata*, birds are counted at the colony sites. Pairs are counted if associated with a nest. Single birds are counted as a prospective pair if sitting on nests, such that all counts represent pairs.

In the 2004 season, ground counts commenced on 30 September. Counting then continued on 3-6-8-10 October. One re-count was made of a small group on 18 October. Counts on consecutive days were not possible due to poor weather conditions. In some areas, counts were made by two observers who worked independently of each other. In such cases an average figure is given. In the 2006 season, ground counts were made of selected areas on 29 September, with a re-check on 2 October. With the aerial survey methodology proving to be more accurate, ground counts were reduced in the 2006 survey to selected areas.

Aerial Surveys

The aerial survey in the 2004 season was carried out on 29 September along the west cliff colonies (Fig. 1 and 4). Photographs were taken from the open door of a Sea King helicopter. Two cameras were used, a medium format Rollei SLX and a Canon EOS10D digital camera of 8.5 mega pixels.

Weather conditions were ideal with a light NW wind and a slightly overcast sky producing a good, even light. The sea was calm. Two separate runs were made along the areas to be surveyed enabling the two cameras to be used in turn by the one surveyor. Flights were made at 70 knots at an average height of 200 m. At this height observations and photographs were made looking down at the nest sites. Keeping a distance of 400m from the cliffs these positions gave a clear view of all birds including nests on deeply inset ledges. The combination of height and distance was also the optimum for the focal lengths used by both cameras.

In the survey carried out on 27 September 2006, exactly the same route, height and distance was followed. The weather was slightly overcast with a SSW wind and broken sea. On this occasion a Sikorsky S61N helicopter was used with two operators photographing from the open cargo door. One run was made at 75 knots. Two cameras were used, a Canon EOS 1D (16 mega pixel) and a Canon EOS 5D (12.5 mega pixel)

Photographs were printed on photo quality paper to Super A3 size, resulting in high quality images. With this imagery, individual birds are clearly shown, enabling single birds on a nest to be identified from pairs. Single birds are counted as a prospective pair, such that all counts represent pairs. Photographs were overlapped to ensure areas were fully covered. Prints were marked to show overlap positions. Three methods were used for counting birds shown on the photographs: In the one, an overlay of transparent film was laid on the print and birds marked off with a fine point marker. A second method was to use two sheets of heavy weight white paper and mask off the photograph to allow either vertical or horizontal strips of the picture to be displayed. The birds in that strip were then counted and noted. Marking the position of the counted strip on the photograph, one sheet of paper was moved over the counted strip, butting precisely with the second, this second sheet was moved to expose another section of the photograph. Sheets were then secured with low tack masking tape. Counts of sections were made until the entire photograph had been covered. Depending on the density of birds, exposed sections of the photograph varied in size to facilitate counting. Where the image of a bird was less than 1mm^2 on a photograph, a photo lupe was used to ensure accuracy. The third method, generally used for counting very dense colonies, employed a PC screen. This method was employed solely for the 2006 survey. Digitised images are overlaid with a grid and individual birds on nests marked off with a brush tool, with total counts in each grid square registered. In the 2006 survey, the results of the two operators, using different focal lengths, were independently assessed. The quality of images and count results were found to be highly correlated.

Comparison between aerial photograph survey and ground count of the Settlement Rookery:

In order to compare the methods, counts were made from an aerial photograph of the Settlement Rookery. Because some sections of the rookery were not covered in the 2004 survey photographs, or were obscured by dense Tussac grass, some ground counts were added. Separate ground and aerial photography counts were made of birds on South Cliff (Fig. 1), a part of Settlement Colony, which formed since 1986. Birds nesting on the West Cliffs could only be successfully counted using aerial photography methods.

Breeding success and comparative counts from other islands:

Fledging success of chicks was determined eight times during the period at New Island. The breeding success at New Island was determined as the number of chicks were close to fledging (in late March-early April) per prospecting/laying pair observed (in late September-early October).

Aerial surveys of North Island (5 miles to the north of New Island) were carried out in conjunction with the New Island surveys. Aerial surveys were also made of Bird Island which is located 35 miles to the SE of New Island. These were made in 2005 and 2006 on the same date as the New Island surveys.

The 1983 count on South Jason (Fig. 2) was made by a ground survey fairly early in the season (9 September), but it was noted that birds were more advanced in nest building than birds on the New Island colonies. A figure of 15% was however added to the ground count to cover late arrivals to this site. This percentage was based on observations of the New Island colonies.

Results
Population Trend

Over 29 years the number of Black-browed albatrosses in the Settlement Rookery in total, and in The Bowl, increased from 998 pairs to 2,001 pairs; a 100.5% increase (Fig. 3) or an average of 3.5% per annum.

Since the last complete survey of the Settlement Rookery in September-October 2000, the population has shown an increase from 1,849 pairs to 2,001 pairs (Table 1 & 2). The counts of The Bowl and the Settlement Rookery total were closely and highly statistically significantly correlated (Fig. 3, R=0.935, N=8, P<0.001).

An aerial survey in October 2000 for the West Cliff area resulted in a total figure of 2,605 pairs. The total of 4,323 in 2006 thus indicates an increase of 1,718 pairs (40%) over 6 years, or an average of 6.6% per annum.

2004 Aerial and Ground Surveys

The counts of the areas of the Settlement Rookery are given in Table 1. The two methods resulted in comparable results (error 34 pairs/1,717 pairs or <2%). The average between aerial and ground count methods was 1,700.

At South Cliff, a total of 166 pairs were counted on the ground in late October, while the aerial survey photographs showed a total of 179 pairs. The average for South Cliff obtained from the two methods was 173 pairs, giving a total for the Settlement Rookery plus birds on South Cliff of 1,890 pairs.

The total number of pairs present in the West Cliffs was 3,324 (Table 2), therefore the total count for the New Island South reserve was 5,214 pairs for 2004.

2006 Aerial and Ground Surveys

The aerial survey was carried out on 27 September 2006 of the same areas covered in the 2004 survey. As aerial and ground counts had been shown to be highly comparable in the 2004 and 2005 surveys (29 September 2005 survey is not detailed in this work) ground counts were limited in this survey to specific areas of the Settlement Rookery. With the very detailed imagery now possible through the use of high quality digital cameras, with errors of less than 1% (established from the results of two sets of photo imagery by two operators) the preference, since the 2004 surveys, is for aerial photography survey methodology.

The total number of pairs counted on the Settlement Rookery, plus birds on the South Cliff, was 2,001, an increase of 111 pairs over the 2004 census.

The total number of pairs recorded on the West Cliffs was 4,323, with a total for New Island South reserve of 6,324 pairs in 2006; an increase of 1,110 pairs (17.5%) over the 2004 census.

Fledging Success

Year	% Fledging Success
1978/79 (Settlement Rookery)	48%
1995/96	56%
2000-2001 (Settlement Rookery)	52%
2002-2003	55%
2003-2004	49%
2004-2005	45%
2006-2007	55%

All figures based on nest attendance at commencement of egg laying, and are for The Bowl area of the Settlement Rookery only, unless stated otherwise.

Comparative counts from other islands
- South Jason Island

Black-browed albatross on this island were counted four times since 1983. There were 366 pairs in 1983. In 1989, an aerial survey showed 950 pairs. Falklands Conservation made a ship-based count in November 2000 of 1,745 pairs, which was consistent with a count of 835 chicks made by the author on 22 January 2001. In September 2005 an aerial survey by the author revealed 1,550 birds on nests, an increase of 26% since 1983, but a decrease based on the count made by Falkland Conservation in November 2000.

- North Island

Four aerial surveys have been carried out, the results of two are given. There were 14,625 pairs in September 1995 and 17969 pairs in September 2004, an 18.6% population increase.

In 2000 Falkland Conservation carried out a ground count with a total of 16,787 (Huin 2000) for the main east side colony. This survey recorded two smaller colonies on the south and northwest cliffs, numbering 250 and 700 respectively. In 1995 the population was confined to the east coast of this island only, thus, between 1995 and 2000, birds have developed new colonies on the west side of North Island which have not been recorded before. In September 2005 an aerial survey of the west side of North Island was carried out with a total of 2,325 birds on nests being recorded, an increase of 1,375 pairs over the figure recorded in 2000. The inclusion of the two colonies counted in 2000, plus those recorded in December 2004, shows that the total population for North Island has increased. Preliminary data in preparation for surveys in 2005 and 2006 of all the colonies on North Island indicate substantial increases, which are in line with the New Island results.

- Bird Island

Several aerial surveys of this site have been made by the author. For comparison with the New Island surveys, the results of two of these are given. Both were carried out on the same dates as New Island surveys on 29 September 2005 and 27 September 2006. The same methodology was employed, but no ground counts were made. In 2005 a total of 12,688 of birds on nests were

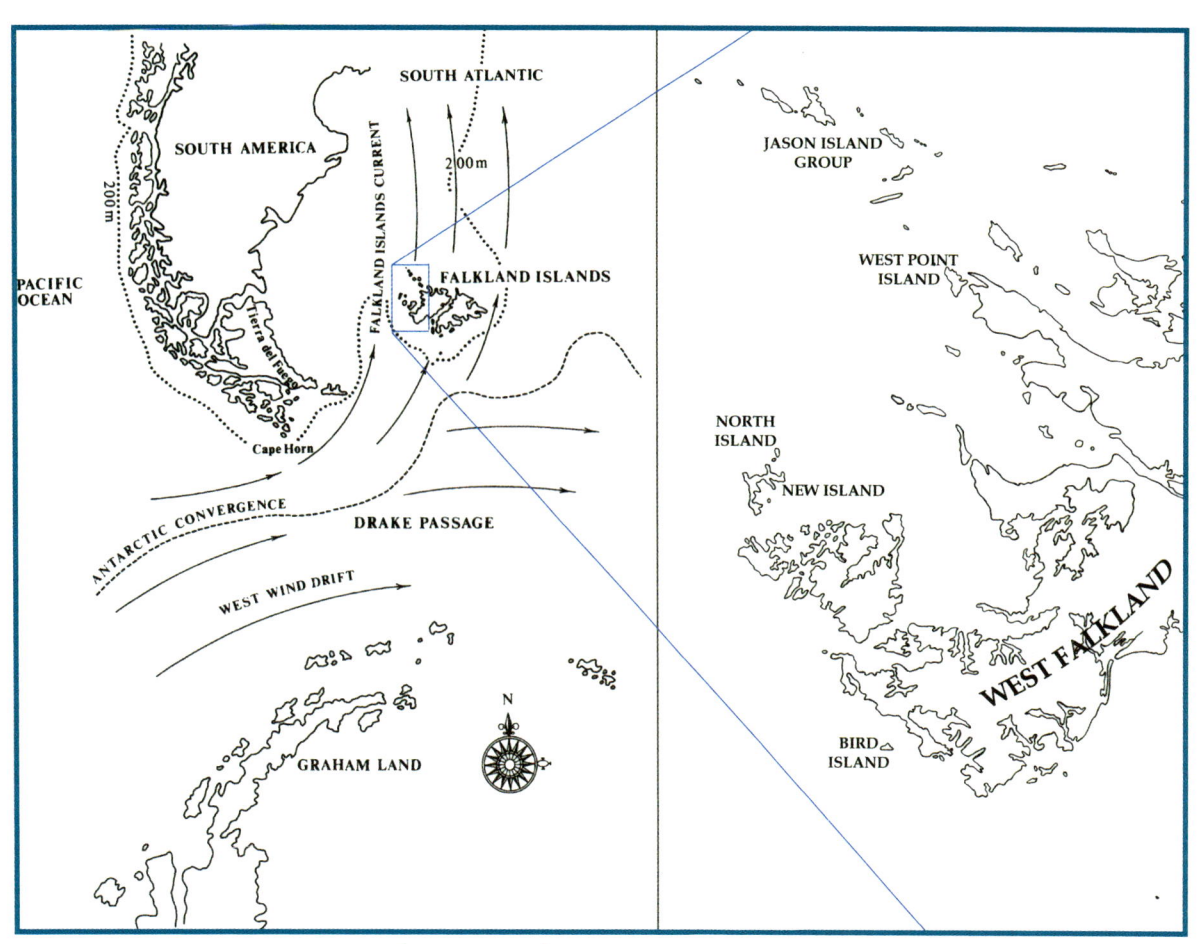

Fig. 2: *Location of New Island (51° 43' S, 061° 17'W), Falkland Islands, with a schematic diagram of the islands in westernmost part of the Falklands Archipelago.*

counted. In the 2006 survey, the total was 15,616 birds on nests, an increase of 2928 or 18.7%.

In November 2000 a ground survey was carried out and a total of 10,189 birds on nests was recorded (Huin, Falkland Conservation Newsletter) The 2005 census detailed above therefore shows an increase of 2,499 pairs, or 19.7%, in the five years since 2000.

Discussion

The data presented here on the Black-browed albatross population of the Settlement Rookery has been collected for the last 29 years and as such is the only data set existing from the Falkland Islands covering such a significant period of time.

In contrast to the overall decline trends reported for the Falkland Islands (Falkland Conservation), but in line with recent studies for other regions in the world (Macquarie Island, see: Terauds et al., 2005), the present long-term data from New Island indicates that the population has been increasing since 1978 (Fig. 3).

The data show a significant and steady increase of this population over the last 29 years where the number of breeding birds has more than doubled. The more recent aerial surveys of the west cliffs of New Island, in 2005, (not detailed in this report) and 2006 also show substantial increases in this population.

Records of dead or dying adult Black-browed albatross on the New Island South Settlement Colony are extremely rare. There are records of only two adult birds found dead in the 29 years of surveys. In the 2002-2003 breeding season a total of two adult birds were discovered dead on the colony, with sightings of others at sea. These deaths, although not proven, may have contributed to the slightly reduced increase between the census of 2000 and 2004.

Situated on the extreme west side of the archipelago, New Island is one of twelve sites in the Falkland Islands which hold breeding populations of Black-browed albatross. Data from New Island on population increase trends are supported also by survey figures from North Island which lies some five miles north of New Island. Three aerial surveys were carried out on the North Island populations on the same dates and show that breeding populations on these sites are increasing.

Figures for South Jason Island also show this trend. In conjunction with aerial surveys of New Island and North Island in 2005 and 2006, aerial surveys were also made of Bird Island which lies some 35 miles SE of New Island, where substantial increases are recorded.

Increases in the Black-browed albatross population at West Point Island, lying 50 km to the north of New Island are also reported (R.B. Napier, pers. comm. 2004). Increases are also reported at Saunders Island, lying 60km to the north east of New Island (D. Pole-Evans, pers. comm. 2004).

The expansion of trawl fishery, in particular, may be associated with an increase in albatross numbers. Scavenging from trawlers may lead to a local increase in food availability (Thompson, 1992; Thompson and Liddy, 1995), by providing novel prey species to albatrosses in the form of pelagic-demersal fish not otherwise available to them. As much as 15% of Black-browed Albatrosses' total food requirements during chick rearing originated as discards from trawlers between 1987 and 1991 (Thompson, 1992). However food in the form of discards during the chick rearing period changes and is very dependent on when a fishery is active. Samples of feed taken in the chick rearing period on New Island in the 2006-2007 season, produced no evidence of fishery discard. Also, it should be noted that the fishery in the area of the Falkland Islands did not commence until 1985, so scavenging from trawlers was not an option for this population before this date.

Data from Steeple Jason Island (Falkland Conservation) show substantial decreases in the breeding population at that site. Steeple Jason Island lies some 70 miles to the NW of New Island. These findings on what is one of the Falklands largest and most dense breeding sites, and the results presented in this paper, offer a new dimension to the question of declining albatross populations.

If there are apparent declines in some areas, with increases in others, this may be due to a percentage of some larger breeding populations moving between sites, and future work should identify such processes and possible causes.

Food availability may be one reason, but site preference, the need for albatross to have access to nest building materials, in particular mud, clay and water, with the possible competition for such things, has to be considered.

Infestations by parasites, particularly in very dense colonies, could also be a factor. For example, Baker et al. (2002) noted that ticks on adults and chicks at colonies of Black-browed albatrosses on the Falkland Islands are known to spread an avian pox virus, causing localised sporadic mortality. Lesions, believed to have been caused by an avian virus, were found on a number of young Black-browed albatross during a banding program on West Point Island in 1963-64 (Napier and Strange, pers. observ.). Other threats identified to affect albatross include for example: direct mortality as by-catch from long-line; trawl and gillnet fishing; dependence upon fisheries discards; over-extraction of prey species; marine pollution; marine debris; alien pest species on land; and avian parasites and diseases (Baker et al. 2002).

Two satellite-tracking studies of Black-browed albatrosses have been carried out in the Falklands, which demonstrated that adults forage mainly over continental shelves (Grémillet et al. 2000; Huin, 2002). Huin (2002) found that during the post-guard period, foraging areas are restricted mainly to the Falkland Island Conservation Zone; the main areas utilised by birds from Saunders Island in the north-west of the Falkland Islands were close to the north and north-west coast of the Falkland Islands, while birds from Beauchêne Island had a complementary distribution, remaining to the south and south-west of the Falkland Islands, with no forays to the north.

The use of mutually exclusive foraging areas may be part of a strategy to minimise intra-specific competition. In 1987-1991, Black-browed albatross from New Island took substantially more fish and lobster krill than birds at either Beauchêne Island or Steeple Jason Island (Thompson 1992), indicating that the oceanographic factors and fisheries distribution in the extreme west of the archipelago may differ from those in the south and north. In addition, the difference in distribution, diet and population trends all suggest that different parts of the large population of Black-browed albatross in the Falkland Islands should be monitored more carefully. There is also a need to re-evaluate some of the small number of early base line data sets on which present day reports of declining Black browed albatross stocks are based. With the development in recent years of digital imagery, aerial photographic survey methodology would be a more accurate survey tool for the Islands' albatross colonies.

A Comparative Study:
The Southern Giant Petrel *Macronectes giganteus* in the Falkland Islands

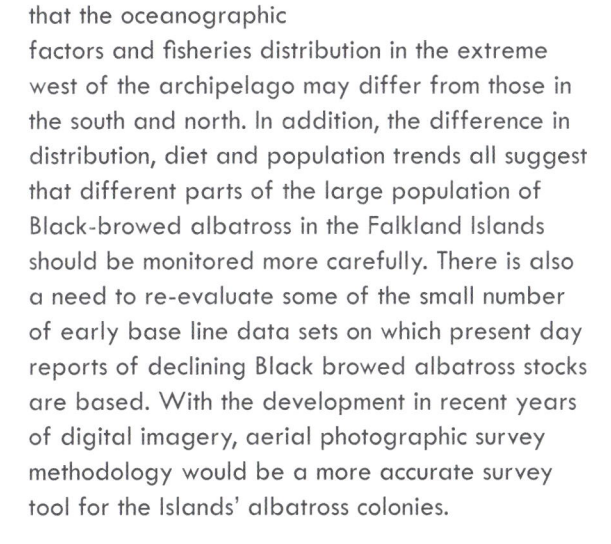

In line with the results presented here, substantial increases in the breeding population of the Southern Giant Petrel *Macronectes giganteus*, is evident in the Falkland Islands.

An estimate for the breeding population of this species between 1978-82 (I. Strange, pers. observ.) gave a total figure of 3,000 breeding pairs for the Falkland Islands.

A ground survey of a breeding colony on Penn Island, 6 miles SE of New Island made in December 1986, gave 900 birds on nests (I. Strange, pers. observ.) An aerial photographic survey of the same site in November 2004 (E. Andersen, pers. comm.) gave a figure of 1,686 birds on nests.

A ground survey of a colony on Third Passage Island in February 1987 found between 70-80 well-developed young, with an estimate of the adult breeding population of 200 breeding pairs (I. Strange, pers. observ.).

In November 2004, an aerial photographic survey of this site produced a figure of 428 birds on nests (E. Andersen, pers. comm.).

Between November 2004 and March 2005, Falkland Conservation (Huin & Reid) carried out an all-Island survey of this species with a total breeding population estimate of 19,810 breeding pairs, with the 2004 figures for Penn Island and Third Passage Island (E. Andersen, unpubl. data) being significantly correlated.

Data obtained shows that between 1982 and 2004, the population of this species has significantly increased by some 85% (an average of 3.8% per annum).

Acknowledgements
A considerable number of people have contributed to fieldwork over a number of years on the New Island South Reserve. Special thanks go to the following for their help in past surveys, the late Ingrid W Schenk for producing the first survey maps. Mary Ann Lea, Sam Thalmann, Stuart McKay, Monica Silva, Petra Quillfeldt, Juan F. Masello and Paulo Catry for surveys, technical assistance and contributing to manuscript. Amy van Buren for recount checks on aerial photographs. Georgina Strange for the production of survey images.

Table 1. *Census of Black-browed Albatrosses of the Settlement Rookery, New Island, September-October 2004. The combined method uses an aerial photograph and ground counts for those areas which are either not covered in the photograph, or are obscured by dense Tussac*

Area	Combined count	Ground count
Area covered by aerial photograph	1102	
A	148	148
B	87	87
C	59	59
E	16	16
F	27	27
G	7	7
K		168
L		120
N		78
O-1	138	138
O-2		476
P	59	59
Q	40	40
Area between gulch		294
TOTAL	1,683	1,717*

* Total including South Cliff (See Table 2) is 1,890

Table 2. *Census of Black-browed Albatrosses of the West Cliff colonies, New Island, September-October 2004*

Area	Count	Remarks
Landsend Bluff	1211	Total three photographs
Mainland Landsend Bluff		Count of 172 birds. See note**
North side Cave Bluff	43	
Cave Entrance area	494	
Cliff south of Cave Entrance	338	
Cliff area at Small Cave	265	
South of Small Cave	90	
Headland north of Dark Cliffs	408	(Dark Cliff area devoid of birds)
Cliffs south of Dark Cliffs	120	
Cliffs	55	
Cliffs	86	
Cliffs north of Rookery Hill	28	
Rookery Hill north	89	Coastal cliffs adjacent to Rookery Hill
Rookery Hill	62	
West Cliffs Settlement Rookery	35	Small area at back of Settlement Rookery
South Cliff		(Total 173 included in Settlement Rookery)
TOTAL	3,324	

**In the 2000-2001 survey, this area was not included. For a comparison with the 2004 survey results, the count of 172 birds is therefore excluded.

Fig. 3: *Population trends for the Settlement Rookery over the last 29 years. Surveys were not possible every season, averaging one every two years. Where total counts are given, figures include the smaller colony known as "The Bowl". The separate survey figure for The Bowl is given to show the population trends of this particular group. Being a relatively small group of birds situated in an ideal location for counting, figures can be considered to be accurate to a point of 1%.*

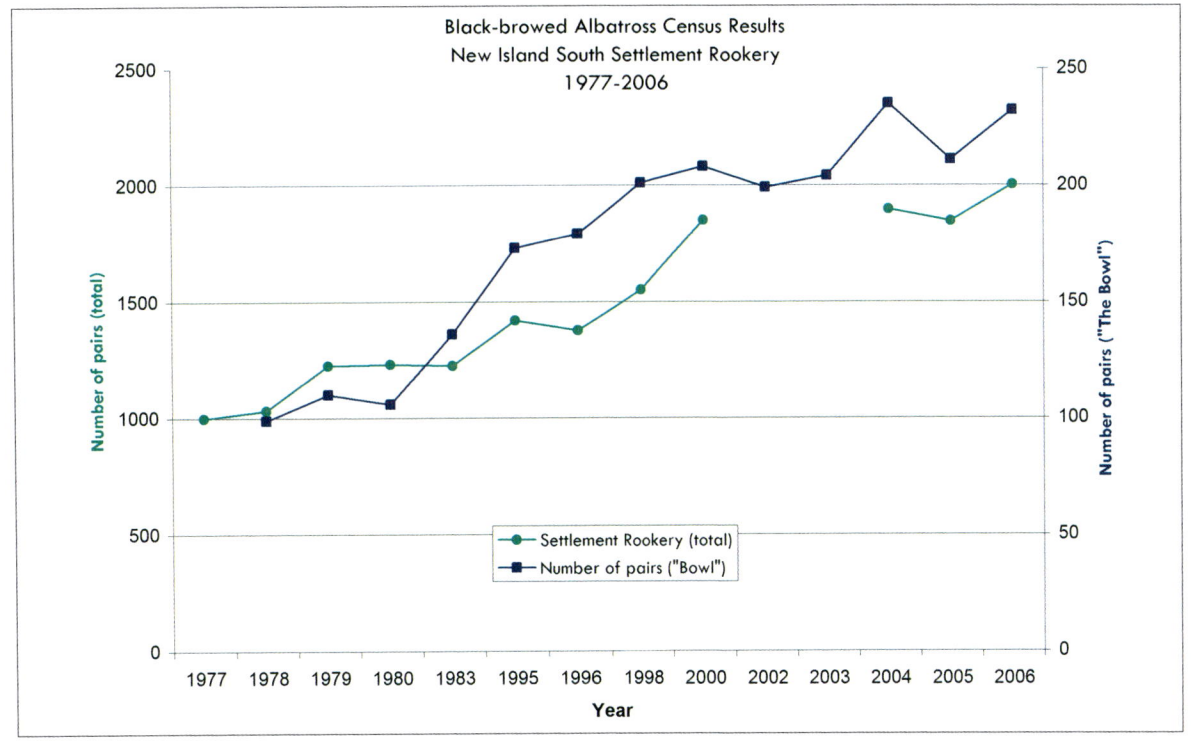

Fig. 4: *Aerial view of the west coastal cliffs of New Island, Falkland Islands*

Annex 6

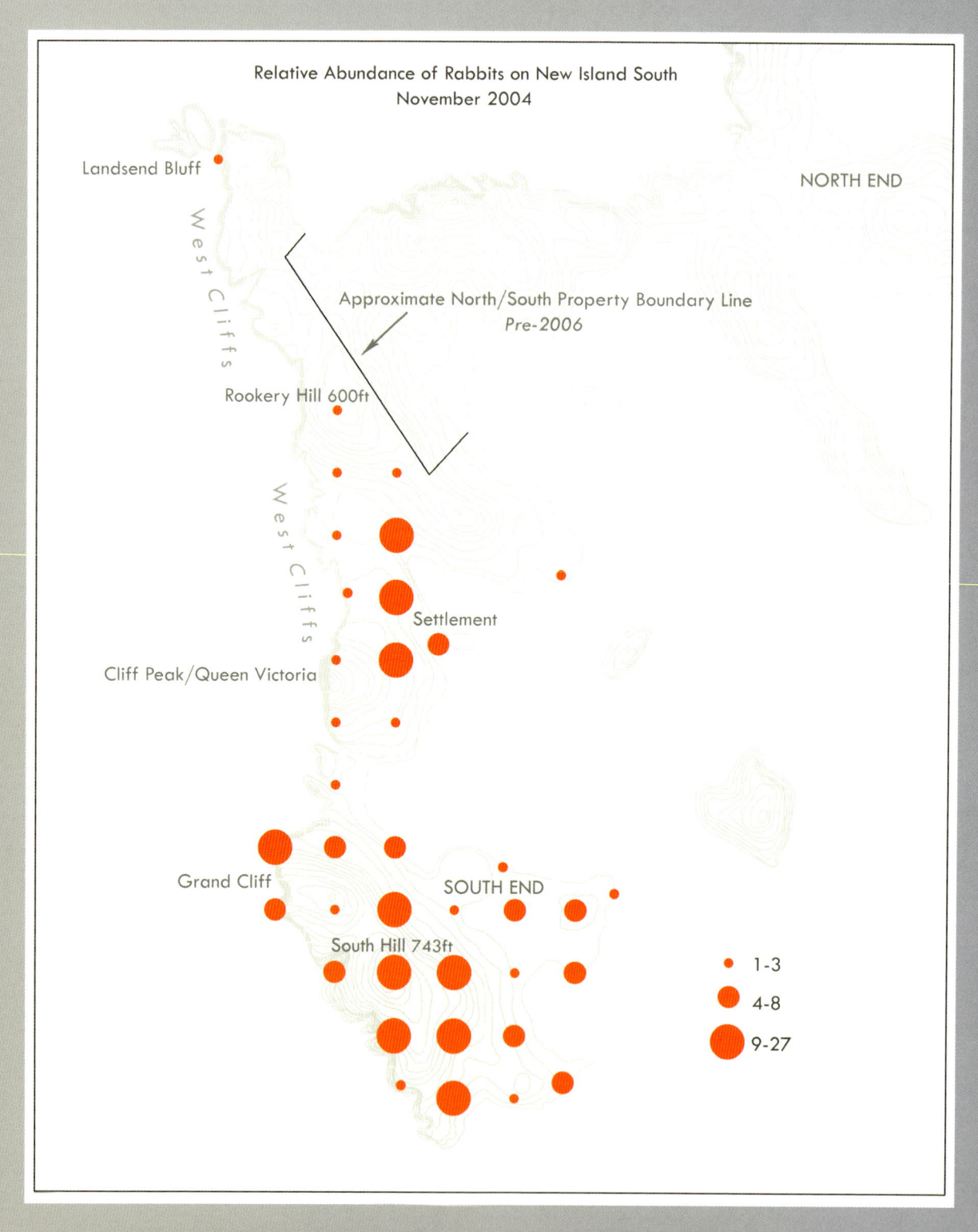

**Relative Abundance of Rabbits on New Island South
November 2004**

Distribution of rabbits on New Island South: number of individuals seen in 20 minute visits to 500x500m-squares. All visits were carried out between 17 October and 17 November 2004. Carried out by Dr Paulo Catry.

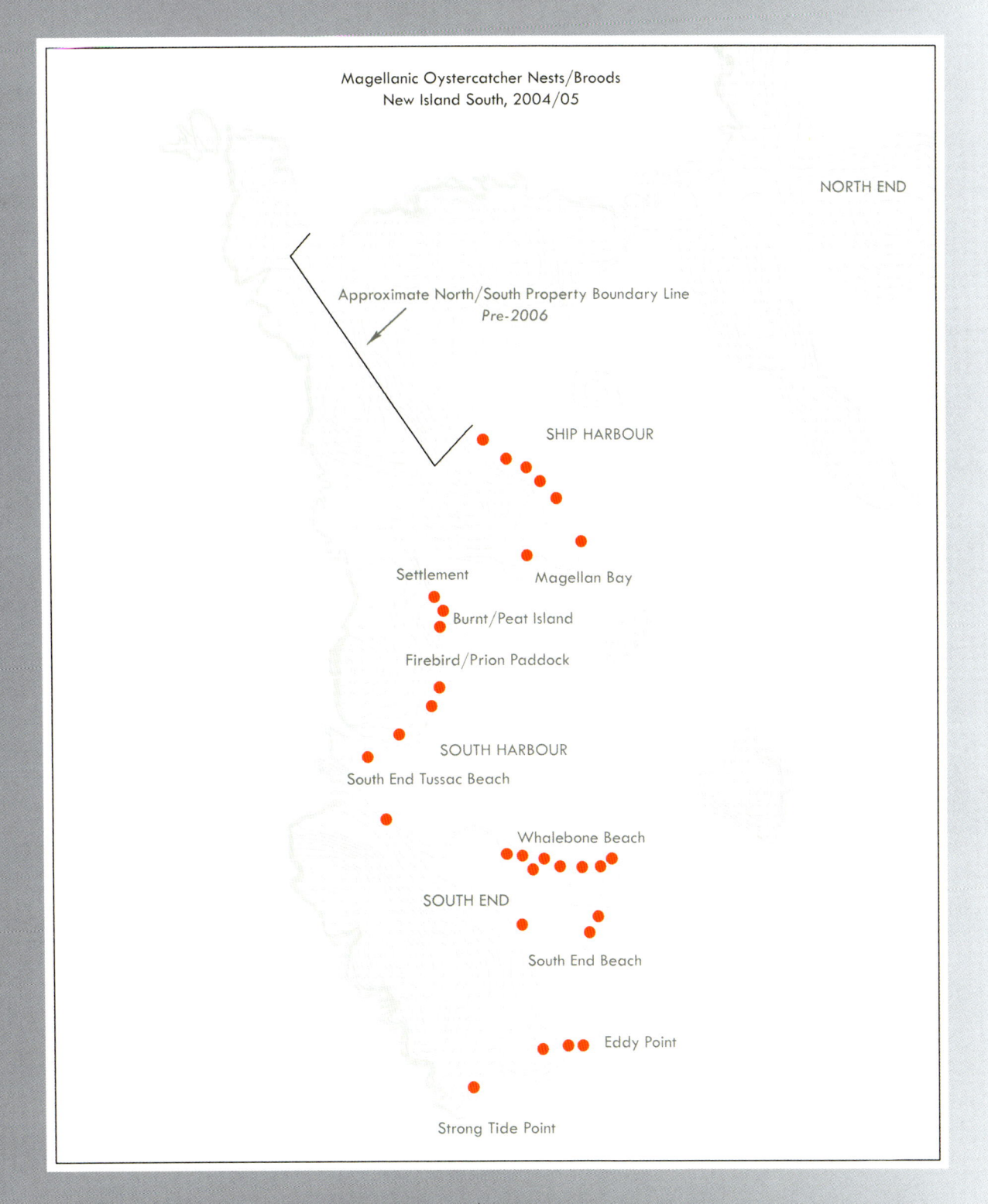

Distribution of Magellanic Oystercatcher nests/broods on New Island South: results from a detailed survey in October-December 2004 carried out by Dr Paulo Catry.

Annex 7

Research carried out on New Island South 1975-2007

A number of professionals and field workers have carried out a variety of research projects over the years. Not all of it has resulted in published works but studies have none the less contributed to our overall knowledge of the island's biodiversity. (For publications see Annex 8).

Early contacts from Europe included Dr Pierre Devillers and Jean Terschuren of the Institut Royal des Sciences Naturelles (Brussels) in 1975/76. Under the auspices of the same Institute, Marie-Odile Beudels and Didier Vangeluwe visited the island in 1992 to carry out population census of many breeding species, with particular emphasis on population dynamics of skuas.

Several groups and individuals from The Netherlands worked on New Island in the 1970s and 80s. Caroline Scholten carried out studies on Magellanic penguins, a group led by Dr H. van Bohemen surveyed New Island in 1979, and Y. de Roever (1978) also surveyed various aspects of the island's bird life.

Dr B. and Dr H. Gerhardt of Germany (1981) carried out comprehensive studies on lichens, leaving a named collection on the island. Educational material on Chloephaga geese was produced following a visit by members of the Zoologischen Garten, Wuppertal, Germany in the late 1970s.

Research on optical performance of the penguin eye took place on Rockhopper penguins in 1980: this was done by Dr J. G. Sivak, Laboratory of Comparative Optometry, University of Waterloo, Ontario (Canada).

Kate Thompson, assisted by Dan Hale, worked on various seabird research projects in 1986/87. Dr Thompson subsequently published various seabird monitoring reports for the Falkland Islands Foundation (later Falklands Conservation).

Timothy Lamey of the University of Oklahoma, USA worked on rockhopper penguin research from 1998, spending three seasons on New Island, while Cammie Sykes Lamey carried out a field study of sibling aggression and nestling mortality in brown skuas. A study was also begun on Gentoo penguins, to assess the ability of birds laying more than a single clutch of eggs. Colleen Cassady St Clair and Bob St Clair, also from Oklahoma University, carried out further work on Rockhopper penguins in 1993/94.

During the period 1997-2004 the New Island Reserve and the University of Washington, Seattle, USA, operated a joint project satellite tracking penguins, under the direction of Prof P. Dee Boersma. Monica C. Silva, Kelly Flynn and Amy van Buren contributed to this research. (See also Pg. 48-49).

The late Ingrid Schenk spent three seasons working on the reserve carrying out vegetation surveys, seabird surveys and instigated the first field studies on rodents. In 1996 Jeanie Vesall also carried out vegetation surveys, developing the islands first herbarium.

Long term studies on Thin-billed prions began in 1998 with Monica C. Silva from University of Washington, Seattle. Jose Pedro Granadeiro contributed to the project in 1998. Research on this species is ongoing [see Pg. 54-55] under Dr Petra Quillfeldt.
Dr Quillfeldt's team now includes PhD student Riek van Noordwijk working on cormorants [see Pg. 57] and Maud Poisbleau, assisted by Laurent Demongin, carrying out a postdoctoral study on Rockhopper penguins [see Pg. 49].

Long term studies were commenced on Upland Geese in 2005 by Anja Gladbach and David Gladbach [see Pg. 59]. Both are PhD students from Germany, working in co operation with Dr Petra Quillfeldt's team.

Dr Paulo Catry's team from Portugal has been involved for some years on wide-ranging research on the island's biodiversity. The group has included Ana Campos, Rafael Matias, Miguel Lecoq and Ana Dias, with assistance from Orea Anderson from Queen's University, Belfast (For details on Dr Catry's work on Black-browed Albatross, see Pg. 52).

Mention must also be made of two seasons valuable field work on rodents carried out by Fabiana Zuniga Olavarria with assistance from Matthew Strange and Shona Strange.

Photos below: Some of the researchers who have spent time studying on New Island...
Clockwise from top left: David & Anja Gladbach working with Upland geese; Ana Campos & Paulo Catry with their son Jaime at the rookery; (L-R) Petra Quillfeldt & her daughter Katja, Laurent Demongin, Riek van Noordwijk, Juan Masello and Maud Poisbleau at the Geoffrey C Hughes Field Station; Miguel Lecoq working with a Black-browed Albatross

Annex 8

Published Science Papers, Reports and Books based on Research conducted on the New Island Reserve

Boersma PD, Stokes DL, Strange IJ, (2002). *Applying ecology to conservation: tracking breeding penguins at New Island South reserve, Falkland Islands.* Aquatic Conservation: Marine and Freshwater Ecosystems 12: 63-74.

Catry P, Silva MC, MacKay S, Campos A, Masello J, Quillfeldt P & Strange IJ, (2006). *Can thin-billed prions Pachyptila belcheri breed successfully on an island with introduced rats, mice and cats? The case of New Island, Falkland Islands.* Polar Biology.

Catry P, Matias R, Lecoq M, (2005). *Bird Report, New Island South Nature Reserve, 2004/05 summer season.* New Island South Conservation Trust, Report.

Catry P, Campos A, (2004). *Bird Report, New Island South Nature Reserve, 2003/04 summer season.* New Island South Conservation Trust, Report.

Catry P, Campos A, Segurado P, Silva M, Strange IJ, (2003). *Population census and nesting habitat selection of thin-billed prion Pachyptila belcheri on New Island, Falkland Islands.* Polar Biology 26: 202-207.

Devillers P and Terschuren JA, (1978). *Relationships between the Blue-eyed Shags of South America.* Le Gerfaut – De Giervalk: 68: 53-86.

Devillers P, (1978). *Distribution and Relationships of South American Skuas,* Le Gerfaut – De Giervalk: 68: 374 – 417.

Devillers P, (1977). *Comments on Plumages and Behaviour of Scoresby's Gull,* Le Gerfaut – De Giervalk: 67: 254-265.

Devillers P, and Terschuren JA, (1976). *Some Distributional Records of Migrant North American Charadriiformes in Coastal South America (Continental Argentina, Falkland Islands, Tierra del Fuego, Chile and Ecuador),* Le Gerfaut – De Giervalk: 66 : 107-125.

Hoerschelmann H, Figge K, (1979). *Organochlorpestizide und polychlorierte Biphenyle in Vogeleiern von den Falklandinseln und aus Norddeutschland,* Environmental Pollution, Applied Science Publishers Ltd., Essex, England.

Keymer IF, Malcolm HM, Hunt A & Horsley DT, (2001). *Health evaluation of penguins (Sphenisciformes) following mortality in the Falklands (South Atlantic).* Diseases of Aquatic Organisms 45: 159-169.

Lamey CS, (1995). *Chick loss in the Falkland skua Catharacta skua antarctica.* Ibis 137: 231-236.

Lamey TC, (1993). *Territorial aggression, timing of egg loss and egg size differences in rockhopper penguins Eudyptes chrysocome on New Island, Falkland Islands.* Oikos 66: 293-297.

Lamey T, (1990). *Hatch Asynchrony and Brood Reduction in Penguins,* Penguin Biology, Academic Press Inc., Edited by LS Davis and JT Darby.

Lea MA, Thalmann S, Vesall J, (1996). *Breeding Status of Bird species on New Island South Reserve.* New Island Project, Report.

Matias R, Catry P (submitted ms). *The diet of feral cats at New Island, Falkland Islands, and possible impacts on breeding seabirds.*

Nolan CP, Strange IJ, Alesworth E, Agnew D, (1998). *A mass stranding of the squid Martialia hyadesi Rochebrunne and Mabille, 1889 (Teuthoidea: Omastrephidae) at New Island, Falkland Islands.* South African Journal of Marine Science 20: 305-310.

Phillips RA, Catry P, Silk J, Bearhop S, McGill F, Afanasyev V, Strange IJ (submitted ms). *Movements, winter distribution and activity patterns of Falkland and brown skuas: insights from loggers and isotopes.*

Quillfeldt P, Masello JF, Strange IJ, (2003). *Breeding biology of the Thin-billed prion Pachyptila belcheri at New Island, Falkland Islands: egg desertion, breeding success and chick provisioning in the poor season 2002/2003.* Polar Biology 26: 746-752.

Quillfeldt P, Strange IJ & Masello JF, (2005). *Escape decisions of incubating females and sex ratio of juveniles in the Upland goose Chloephaga picta.* Ardea 93: 171-178.

Quillfeldt P, Masello JF, Strange IJ & Buchanan KL, (2006), *Begging and provisioning of Thin-billed prions Pachyptila belcheri is related to testosterone and corticosterone.* Animal Behaviour, 71, 1359-1369.

Quillfeldt P, Strange IJ & Masello JF (2007) *Sea surface temperatures and behavioral buffering capacity in Thin-billed prions: breeding success, provisioning and chick begging.* Journal of Avian Biology 38.

Quillfeldt P, Strange IJ, Segelbacher G & Masello JF (in press) *Male and female contributions to provisioning rates of Thin-billed prions Pachyptila belcheri in the South Atlantic.* Journal of Ornithology.

Quillfeldt P, Strange IJ, Masello JF, Gladbach A, Roesch V, Rona AR, McGill & Furness RW, (submitted ms), *Introduced mammals coexist with seabirds at New Island, Falkland Islands, II: Stable isotope analysis of the diet of introduced mammals during the nestling period of Thin-billed prions.*

Reid T, Catry P, (2006). *The white-chinned petrel population of the Falkland Islands.* Falklands Conservation & New Island South Conservation Trust, Report.

Reid T, Lecoq M, Catry P (in press). *The white-chinned petrel Procellaria aequinoctialis population of the Falkland Islands.* Marine Ornithology.

Schenk I, Strange IJ, Masello JF, Quillfeldt P, (submitted ms), *Introduced mammals coexist with seabirds at New Island, Falkland Islands, I: Abundance of rodents and diet of ship rats during the incubation period of Thin-billed Prions.*

Schurer U, (1980). *Beobachtungen an Spiegelgansen (Gattung Chloephaga) des sudlichen Argentinien und der Falklandinseln.*

Splettstoesser JF, (1985). *Note on rock striations caused by penguin feet, Falkland Islands.* Arctic and Alpine Research 17: 107-111.

St Clair CC, (1998). *Multiple mechanisms of reversed hatching asynchrony in rockhopper penguins.* Journal of Animal Ecology 65: 485-494.

Published Science Papers, Reports and Books based on Research conducted on the New Island Reserve, cont'd.

St Clair CC, (1998). *What is the function of first eggs in crested penguins?* Auk 115: 478-482.

St Clair CC, St Clair RC, (1996). *Causes and consequences of egg loss in rockhopper penguins Eudyptes chrysocome.* Oikos 77: 459-466.

Stock JH and Platvoet D, (1991). *The Freshwater Amphipoda of the Falkland Islands.* Journal of Natural History, 1991, 25: 1469-1491. [Dr Harry Smit of the Foundation for Sub Antarctic Research carried out much of the field work on New Island South; his collection enabled the paper to be written].

Strange IJ, (1989). *Albatross Alley.* Natural History 7 (89): 27-32.

Strange IJ, (1980). *The thin-billed prion Pachyptila belcheri, at New Island, Falkland Islands.* Gerfaut 70: 411-445.

Strange IJ, (1982). *Breeding ecology of the rockhopper penguin (Eudyptes crestatus) in the* Falkland Islands. Gerfaut 72: 137-188.

Strange IJ, (1986). *Tussac Grass Survey in the Falkland Islands.*

Strange IJ, (1989). *Conservation and Environmental Assessment Report.* Report for the Falkland Islands Government.

Strange IJ, (1994). *Fur Seal Survey.* Report to Foreign & Commonwealth Office.

Strange IJ, (1996). *The Striated Caracara (Phalcoboenus australis) in the Falkland Islands.* P. Myers Press.

Strange IJ, (2000). *Counting Rockhopper penguins Eudyptes chrysocome Electronically.* New Island South Conservation Trust, Report.

Strange IJ, (2000-2001). *Black-browed Albatross Diomedia melanophris Population Census, New Island South.* New Island South Conservation Trust, Report.

Strange IJ, (2001). *Gentoo Penguin Pygoscelis papua Census on New Island South Reserve.* New Island South Conservation Trust, Report.

Strange IJ, (2004). *Black-browed Albatross Thalassarche melanophrys population census at New Island South, Falkland Islands, September-October 2004, and population trends from 1977 to 2006.* New Island South Conservation Trust, Report.

Voisin JF, (1982). *Observations on the Falkland Islands Giant Petrels Macronectes giganteus solanderi.* Le Gerfaut 72: 367-380.

Voisin JF & Roux P, (1982). *Notes sur les Carabiques des iles Falkland.* Bulletin de la Societe Entomologique de France.

Annex 9

Additional Bibliography and References

Barton J, (2002). *Fisheries and fisheries management in Falkland Islands Conservation Zones.* Aquatic Conservation: Marine and Freshwater Ecosystems 12: 127-135.

Broughton DA & McAdam JH, 2002. *A Red Data List for the Falkland Islands vascular flora.* Oryx 36: 279-287.

Clausen AP & Huin N, 2003. *Status and numerical trends of King, Gentoo and Rockhopper penguins breeding in the Falkland Islands.* Waterbirds 26: 389-402.

Croxall JP, McInnes SJ, Prince PA, (1984). *The status and conservation of seabirds at the Falkland Islands.* In: Croxall JP, Evans PGH, Scheiber RW (eds) *Status and conservation of the World's Seabirds.* ICBP, Cambridge, pp 271-291.

Croxall JP, Prince PA, Baird A, Ward P, (1985). *The diet of the Southern rockhopper penguin Eudyptes chrysocome chrysocome at Beauchêne Island, Falkland Islands.* Journal of Zoology, London. (A) 206: 485-496.

Davies TH, McAdam JH, (1989). *Wild flowers of the Falkland Islands.* Bluntisham Books, Cambridge.

Grémillet D, Wilson RP, Wanless S, Chater T, (2000). *Black-browed albatrosses, international fisheries and the Patagonian Shelf.* Marine Ecology Progress Series 195: 269-280.

Huin N, (2002). *Foranging distribution of the Black-browed Albatross, Thalassarche melanophris, breeding in the Falkland Islands.* Aquatic Conservation: Marine and Freshwater Ecosystems 12: 89-99.

Moore DM, (1968). *The vascular flora of the Falkland Islands.* British Antarctic Survey Scientific Report No 60.

Napier RB, (1968). *Erect-crested and rockhopper penguins interbreeding in the Falkland Islands.* British Antarctic Survey Bulletin 16: 71-72.

O'Gorman F, (1960). *The Fur seal, Arctocephalus australis, on New Is., West Falkland Islands.* Unpublished report.

Piatkowski U, Pütz K, Heinemann H, (2001). *Cephalopod prey of king penguins (Aptenodytes patagonicus) breeding at Volunteer Beach, Falkland Islands, during austral winter 1996.* Fisheries Research 52: 79-90.

Prince PA, (1981). *The Black-browed albatross Diomedea melanophris population at Beauchêne Island, Falkland Islands.* Colloque sur les Ecosystèmes Subantartiques, 1981, Paimpont. C.N.F.R.A. n° 51

Pütz K, Clausen AP, Huin N, Croxall JP, (2003). *Re-evaluation of Historical Rockhopper Penguin Population Data in the Falkland Islands.* Waterbirds 26 (2): 169-175.

Pütz K, Smith JG, Ingham RJ, Lüthi BH, (2003). *Satellite tracking of male rockhopper penguins Eudyptes chrysocome during the incubation period at the Falkland Islands.* Journal of Avian Biology 34: 139-144.

Additional Bibliography & References, cont'd.

Pütz K, Ingham RJ, Smith JG, (2002). *Foraging movements of Magellanic penguins Spheniscus magellanicus during the breeding season in the Falkland Islands.* Aquatic Conservation: Marine and Freshwater Ecosystems 12: 75-87.

Pütz K, Ingham RJ, Smith JG, Lüthi BH, (2002). *Winter dispersal of rockhopper penguins Eudyptes chrysocome from the Falkland Islands and its implications for conservation.* Marine Ecology Progress Series 240: 273-284.

Pütz K, Ingham RJ, Smith JG, Croxall JP, (2001). *Population trends, breeding success and diet composition of gentoo Pygoscelis papua, magellanic Spheniscus magellanicus and rockhopper Eudyptes chrysocome penguins in the Falkland Islands.* Polar Biology 24: 793-807.

Stackpole EA, (1953). *The Sea Hunters.*

Strange IJ, (1992). *A Field Guide to the Wildlife of the Falkland Islands & South Georgia*, HarperCollins, London.

Strange IJ, (1985). *The Falkland Islands and Their Natural History.*

Strange IJ, (1972, 1981, 1983). *The Falkland Islands.* David & Charles, Newton Abbott.

Strange IJ, (1981). *Penguin World.* Dodd Mead, USA.

Strange IJ, (1976). *The Bird Man.* Gordon & Cremonesi, London.

Thompson KR, (1993). *Variation in magellanic penguin Spheniscus magellanicus diet in the Falkland Islands.* Marine Ornithology 21: 57-67.

Thompson D, Strange IJ, Riddy M, & Duck CD, (2005). *The size and status of the population of southern sea lions Otaria flavescens in the Falkland Islands.* Biological Conservation 121: 357-367.

Tickell WLN, (1967). *Movements of Black-browed and Grey-headed Albatrosses in the South Atlantic.* The Emu 66 (4): 357-367.

Tingley G, Saunders G, Harries D & King J, (1996). *The first shallow marine survey around the Falkland Islands.* Report for the Falkland Islands Government on behalf of IC Consultants Ltd (ICON).

Trehearne M, (1978). *Falkland Heritage, A Record of Pioneer Settlement.* A.H. Stockwell Ltd.

Upton J, Shaw CJ, (2002). *An overview of the oceanography and meteorology of the Falkland Islands.* Aquatic Conservation: Marine and Freshwater Ecosystems 12: 15-25.

Usher MB, (1983). *Two spiders in subfamily Mynoglenidae (Aranae: Linyphiidae) from the Falkland Islands, South Atlantic.* Journal of Zoology, London. 200: 549-560.

White RW, Clausen AP, (2002). *Rockhopper (Eudyptes chrysocome chrisocome) and Macaroni (E. chrysolophus) penguin hybrids apparently breeding in the Falkland Islands.* Marine Ornithology 30: 40-42

White RW, Reid JB, Black AD & Gillon KW, (1999). *Seabird and marine mammal dispersion in the waters around the Falkland Islands – 1998-1999.* Joint Nature Conservation Committee, Peterborough.

A pair of Pied Oystercatchers amongst Sea Cabbage

Falkland Thrush (immature)

Annex 10

New Island's Code of Practice for Visitors

The reserve is a refuge for its wildlife, but also for man to enjoy nature without the constraints of notices, board walks, barriers and dictatorial rules. Please assist us by following common sense rules, so these constraints will never have to be imposed. We try to advise, but if you are not sure, please ask. The following are a few simple considerations that we ask you to follow:

- Natural predators, such as Skuas and Striated Caracaras breeding on New Island are quick to learn that human visitors have the potential to disturb birds on their nests, thus assisting their predation. Be very mindful of this when you walk the perimeter of a seabird colony or see geese and other birds on nests - if you accidentally disturb a nesting bird which has eggs or chicks, please move away from the site as quickly as possible so as the bird may return to its nest.

- If you come across litter, please collect and bring to disposal points in the settlement. Pieces of old glass from many decades of human settlement continue to appear and can be a fire risk; please collect, or notify staff of the location.

- Please avoid Prion breeding areas where the ground is very fragile and pitted with small burrows where these petrels make their nests. If you accidentally break the surface of a Prion nest chamber, carefully check to see if an egg or bird is present, and if so, try to re-cover the chamber with a flat stone or suitable material.

- New Island holds one of the few Fur Seal breeding grounds accessible to visitors; Fur seals are both shy and aggressive, so colonies should be observed from a distance and should not be entered.

- New Island has a very low rainfall and is extremely dry in summer, so we have to impose a strict No Smoking policy.

- Take only memories and photographs away. The Falkland Islands have strict codes on the export of environmental material, plants, animal material such as whale bone etc, so please help us comply.

- Areas where Giant petrels nest on the northern part of the island are out of bounds to all persons, including field workers, at all times. Giant petrels will readily desert their eggs if disturbed, even by the mere presence of a distant observer.

- Everyone, including field research staff, is advised to keep away from nesting areas of South American Terns, especially when these birds are nest-building or on eggs. At this stage terns are easily disturbed and can desert.

- Specific requests to tourist vessels are to keep boat activity, i.e. the use of Zodiac-type craft, to essential passenger transport only. Diving is allowed, but no water sports. The collection of seafood such as Mussels from the island's shoreline is not permitted.

- Please don't feed the wildlife - the birds and animals on the reserve are wild; the food we eat is not a natural component of their diet and may do them more harm in the long term.

Map of the Falkland Islands

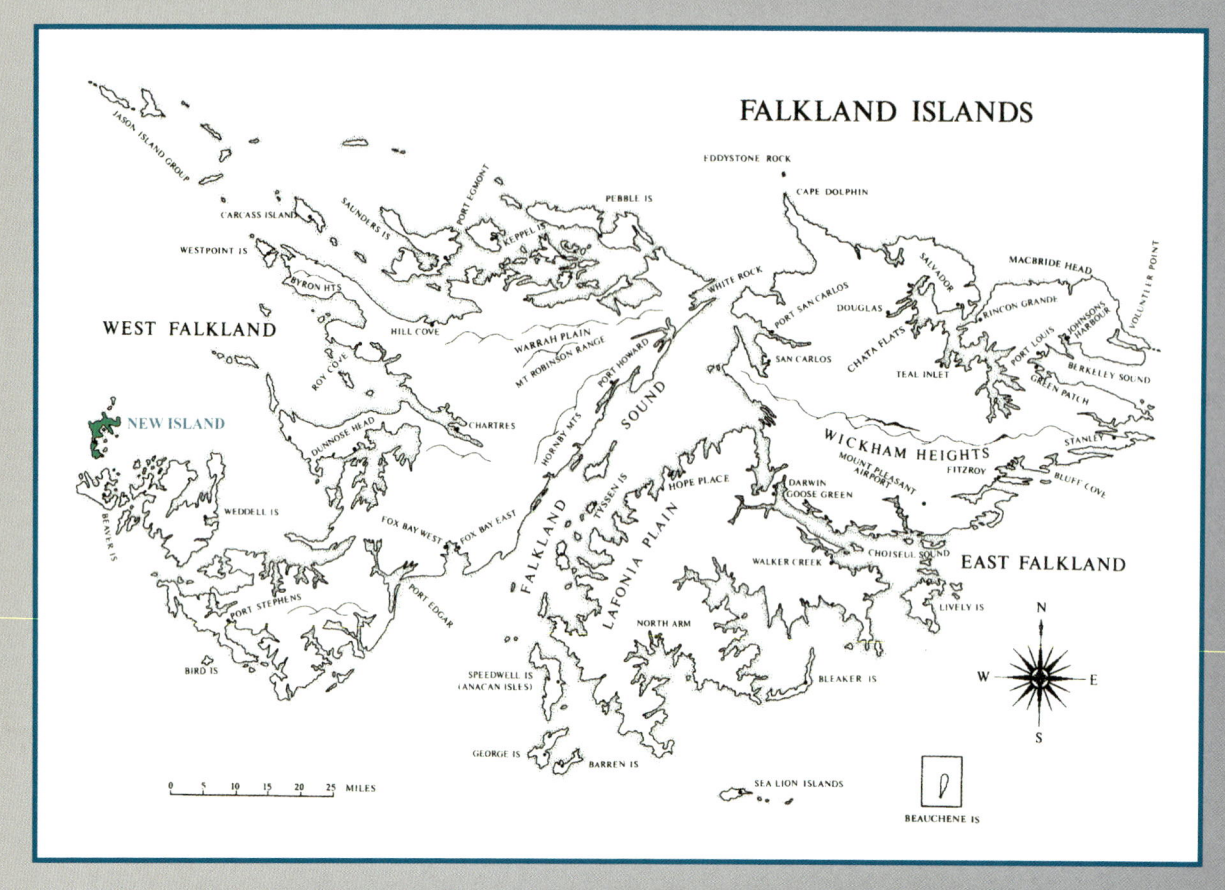

Map of the Falkland Islands, showing New Island in the far west of the archipelago

Photos: Visitors enjoying the view - New Island's Settlement Peak & Grand Cliff; Diddle-dee berries; Dolphin Gulls

Map of New Island

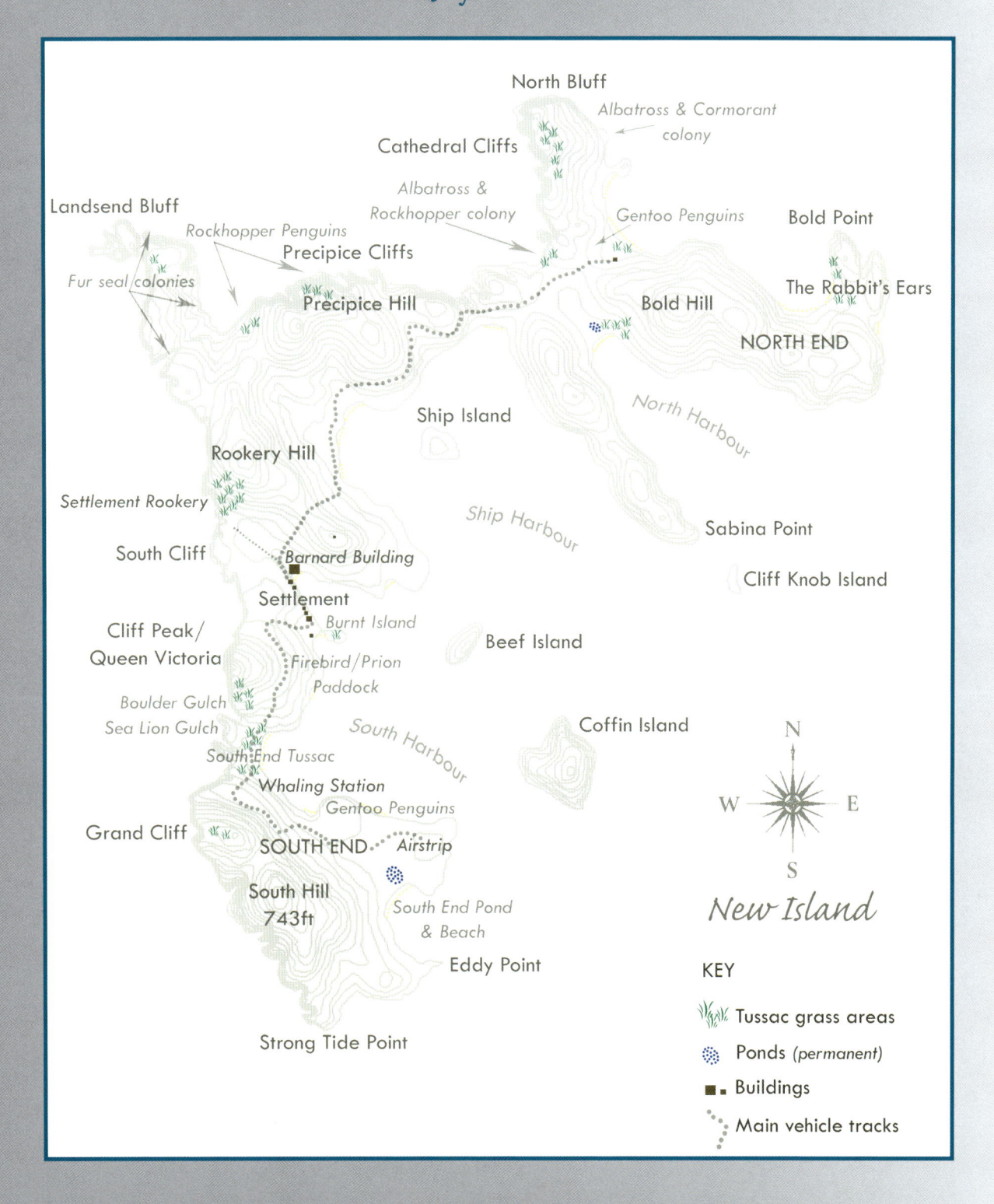

New Island Conservation Trust
Charity Details

The New Island Conservation Trust is a non-profit, charitable conservation organisation

Charity number 1047676
(UK Charity Commission Registered Number)

Contact Details (NICT, UK):
The Secretary
New Island Conservation Trust
Dairy Cottage
Swans Farm
Winchfield
Hook
Hampshire RG27 8DB
England

www.newislandtrust.com

Contact Details
(I. J. Strange, Falkland Islands):
Ian Strange
The Dolphins
Snake Hill
Stanley
Falkland Islands
FIQQ 1ZZ